JUNIOR HIGH BIBLE ACTIVITIES

by
Carol Hillebrenner

illustrated by Ron Wheeler

Cover by Ron Wheeler

Copyright © 1994, Shining Star Publications

ISBN No. 1-56417-009-8

Standardized Subject Code TA ac

Printing No. 987654321

Shining Star Publications
1204 Buchanan St., Box 299
Carthage, IL 62321-0299

Unless otherwise indicated, the New International Version of the Bible was used in preparing the activities in this book.

TABLE OF CONTENTS

88496

Shining Star Publications. Copyright © 1994

SS3831

DEDICATION

"Teach a child how he should live, and he will remember it all his life." Proverbs 22:6 (*TEV)

Thanks, Mom and Dad (Doris Stipp and the late Lloyd Merker), for a good life.

"Her husband puts his confidence in her, and he will never be poor." Proverbs 31:11 (*TEV)

Thanks, Ric, for keeping the faith all these years.

Today's English Version
of the Bible

SS3831

TO THE TEACHER/PARENT

Working with junior highers is truly an exciting, rewarding, and challenging experience. When you win their trust, you'll know the joy of influencing some of God's greatest creations.

The ages of eleven to fourteen are difficult for everyone, especially for the youths who are living through this age of transition. They are uncertain who they are, and where they are going. They are afraid to allow anyone to discover how uncertain they are. This combination can make working with them a frustrating as well as rewarding experience.

What do juniors highers want from you?

Respect. They don't want you to talk down to them or to tell them anything. They don't want a best buddy; that's what their friends are for. They would like an adult interested in them and their concerns. When they know they have your respect, they will respect you. They expect rules, and you can expect them to test those rules on every occasion. They expect you to listen to their problems, but they don't want answers to those problems from your vast experience. They know you did not experience life as they are now experiencing it. Sadly, a lot of them want the impossible: they want someone to make them happy all the time.

What do you want from them?

Respect. You might get it if you earn it. You may also want them to do everything you want them to do when you want it. Forget it!

What will they do for you?

Sometimes they will happily do anything you want. Other times, even the ones you are counting on to help you with a project or discussion will abandon you. This is not because they are being deliberately difficult, but because they are confused by peer pressure or their own personal needs for recognition. If a project or discussion goes well for more than half the group, you deserve to feel a sense of accomplishment.

What will you do for them?

First and foremost, you will help to make God a part of their lives without trying to drive the point home so forcefully that they are turned off by God or religion. With patience and hard work, you will be their adult friend, one of their most powerful links to being grown-ups. You will influence them more by your example than by what you say. It's vitally important that you keep your own bad habits under control because your flaws are as powerful an influence as the good you are trying to do.

What happens when things go badly for them?

If they trust you, they will probably tell you about it. Don't get angry. Maybe it's just not the right time, or they just aren't the right group for the project you wish to do. If most of the group seem interested, you can always put it to a vote. If you lose, try plan B. If the vote is for continuing

 SS3831

the project, you can point out that the majority has spoken, and good sportsmanship means doing one's best not to be difficult. Sometimes a junior higher will resist any suggestions because he has problems you know nothing about.

What happens when things go badly for you?

Always have a plan B and sometimes a plan C in mind. Some days nothing will work with a certain group. Reassess your expectations for them and yourself. We always want everything to work out right, but junior highers aren't underage adults or cuddly children. What they are is people trying to get a life, and they don't yet know what it will be.

SS3831

PERSONAL PROJECTS

The journal (pages 8-14) and bookmark (pages 15-18) may be introduced by explaining that they are like yardsticks to help junior highers measure their relationship to God and to others. Encourage them to accept the challenge of knowing themselves better because this will make it easier to understand others. The Thanks-a-Gram (pages 19-20) will help junior highers see the good in others and share it in a fun way. Point out that you are asking them to be serious and you understand that being serious isn't always easy. Say that you hope they will seriously accept your challenge to know themselves better because you are confident they will find themselves very interesting people.

"GOD AND ME" JOURNAL

Make enough copies of pages 8-14 so that each student will have a journal. Distribute the journals at a youth meeting, possibly near the end of the time you have together. Have each student put his name on the front cover. Assure students that they will never have to show the journals to anyone, although they may do so if they wish. Discuss the idea of privacy to help them understand that it is unfair and unkind for them to look in anyone's journal without permission. They should treat others with the same respect they would like to receive. Make it quite clear that everyone is to respect the privacy of others. Also help students understand that it is not fair to tempt others to look in their journals by leaving them lying around.

The cover of the "God and Me" journal may be copied on colored paper. "What's Happening?" is printed on journal pages 6-7, but the inside cover of the journal may also be used to record ideas, jokes, and interesting things your junior highers have seen and done. You may wish to encourage them to create cover art to make their journals their very own. Discourage illustrations of violence, such as guns, explosions, and knives.

The journal is made from four sheets of 8½" x 11" paper, cropped on the solid cutting lines, folded on the broken lines, and pasted and stapled to create a book measuring 5" x 8½". Pages 1 and 12 are copied on one side of one sheet of paper and pages 2 and 11 are on the opposite side. Pages 3 and 10 are printed on one side of a piece of paper and 4 and 9 on the opposite side. Pages 5 and 8 are printed on one side and 6 and 7 are on the opposite side.

 SS3831

GOD
AND

_____'s

JOURNAL

With God's help, I can do any good thing!

SS3831

YOUR DAILY JOURNAL

Welcome to the world of the private journal! Even before there was a written language, people began recording their thoughts in paintings of animals and people on cave walls. After writing was developed, people recorded their thoughts on clay tablets, animal skins, papyrus, or paper. Some people became famous, and their journals help us know them better. Some writers were just ordinary people, but their journals told so much about life when and where they lived that the authors became famous. Writing in this journal doesn't promise you fame or fortune, but you will get to know yourself better. You will probably find, you are a pretty special person.

The two center pages and front and back covers of your journal are for your thoughts, good jokes, or whatever you see or do that would be fun to remember in the future.

You never need to show any part of this book to anyone unless you want to. You have no right to read the journal of anyone else, and they have no right to read yours. This is what privacy means. Privacy is very important in this day and age when there are so many people and so few ways to have time and space of our own. Respect the rights of others, including their right to privacy, as you would expect them to respect your rights.

1

AUTOGRAPHS

12

Shining Star Publications, Copyright © 1994

SS3831

DAY 8

Visit the imaginary mirror again today. Have there been changes?

I look different on the outside because . . .

I look different on the inside because . . .

The changes I'd like to make to my outside now are . . . .

The changes I'd like to make to my inside now are . . .

Are the changes the same as when you began your journal? If they are different, what happened to make you change your mind?

My hopes for the future are . . . .

With God's help, I can do any good thing.

11

DAY 1

"Know yourself, and your neighbor will not mistake you."
Scottish Proverb

Below are some thoughts about what you think of yourself and others. Be honest. At the end of the journal is another challenge to see if you have grown to understand yourself and your feelings better after you have tried a few days of writing in your personal journal. Place an X or your initial at the point on the scales which most closely indicates how you feel between agreement and disagreement with the statement.

I like being with the kids from my church.

Disagree   Agree
   1   2   3   4   5   6   7   8   9   10

I can make new friends if I try.

Disagree   Agree
   1   2   3   4   5   6   7   8   9   10

People from my church listen to me better than my nonchurch friends.

Disagree   Agree
   1   2   3   4   5   6   7   8   9   10

With people from my church I can really be myself.

Disagree   Agree
   1   2   3   4   5   6   7   8   9   10

I can make mistakes at church without feeling embarrassed.

Disagree   Agree
   1   2   3   4   5   6   7   8   9   10

Someone is happy because I am alive.

Disagree   Agree
   1   2   3   4   5   6   7   8   9   10

I will make an extra effort to be a friend to more people today.

Disagree   Agree
   1   2   3   4   5   6   7   8   9   10

2

SS3831

DAY 2

"It matters not what you are thought to be, but what you are." Publilius Syrus (785 B.C.)

Pretend you are standing in front of a mirror, seeing yourself as others see you. Complete these statements about yourself as honestly as possible.

On the outside I look . . . .

If people could see inside me, they would see . . .

If I could change my outside, I would change . . . .

If I could change my inside, I would change . . . .

My hopes for what will happen when I'm with my friends are . . . .

With God's help, I can do any good thing.

3

DAY 7

Do this without looking back at your first day chart. Make your mark on the scales between agree and disagree. Then look back and see if you've had a change of attitude. Is it for the best? If it isn't, could it be you are expecting more of other people than they can possibly give? Are you giving enough of yourself? Maybe this is something you want to talk about to someone.

I like being with the kids from my church.

Disagree   Agree
1 2 3 4 5 6 7 8 9 10

I can make new friends if I try.

Disagree   Agree
1 2 3 4 5 6 7 8 9 10

People from my church listen to me better than my nonchurch friends.

Disagree   Agree
1 2 3 4 5 6 7 8 9 10

With people from my church I can really be myself.

Disagree   Agree
1 2 3 4 5 6 7 8 9 10

I can make mistakes at church without feeling embarrassed.

Disagree   Agree
1 2 3 4 5 6 7 8 9 10

Someone is happy because I am alive.

Disagree   Agree
1 2 3 4 5 6 7 8 9 10

I will make an extra effort to be a friend to more people today.

Disagree   Agree
1 2 3 4 5 6 7 8 9 10

10

SS3831

DAY 6

The things I did or will do today to help me be nearer God are . . . .

The best part about today is . . .

The thing that I did today that would please God is . . .

My personal prayer for today is . . . .

An old French proverb says, "Be careful what you pray for; you might get it." What does that mean?

9

DAY 3

"'Love the Lord your God with all your heart and with all your soul and with all your mind and with all your strength.' The second is this: 'Love your neighbor as yourself.' There is no commandment greater than these." Mark 12:30-31

Memorize these verses. Considering what they say, complete the following statements.

To me, God is . . .

When I think about giving all my heart, soul, mind, and strength to loving God, I find . . .

To me, my neighbor is . . .

I know those verses mean I should think of all people everywhere as my neighbors, but I . . . .

To be a better neighbor, I should . . . .

4

SS3831

DAY 4

If God spoke to me, I'd like Him to tell me . . .

If I could do anything in the world to help others, I would . . .

The one thing I will try to do today is . . .

The best part about today is . . .

My personal prayer for today is . . . .

5

DAY 5

"A friend loves at all times." Proverbs 17:17a

How important are your friends to you? Do you work at being a better friend? Are you a friend of God?

The person I'd most like to be better friends with is . . .

To be better friends, I should . . . .

The person I think seems to have the best relationship with God is . . .

I think this because . . .

I could be a better friend of God if I would . . .

8

SS3831

WHAT'S HAPPENING?

7

WHAT'S HAPPENING?

6

SS3831

"THINKING IT OUT" BOOKMARKS

Have pens and Bibles on hand for this project. Explain that this is not a test and no one will check answers. The bookmarks are a way for teens to learn more about themselves. Encourage them to keep their bookmarks in their Bibles and every six months check themselves to see how their answers have changed. Ask students to consider if these changes suggest that they are growing more mature in their outlook on life or if they are perhaps allowing their friends to influence them.

The bookmarks may be reproduced on colored paper.

SS3831

WHAT DO I OWE GOD?

Read Matthew 7:1-5, 7-12.

Things to think out:

How fair am I?

Do I judge people by how they look?

Do I judge people by how others feel about them instead of by my true feelings?

Do I know how to help others?

Do I know how to ask for help when I need it?

Is it selfish to ask for help?

WHAT DO I OWE GOD?

Read Matthew 7:1-5, 7-12.

Things to think out:

How fair am I?

Do I judge people by how they look?

Do I judge people by how others feel about them instead of by my true feelings?

Do I know how to help others?

Do I know how to ask for help when I need it?

Is it selfish to ask for help?

WHAT DO I OWE GOD?

Read Matthew 7:1-5, 7-12.

Things to think out:

How fair am I?

Do I judge people by how they look?

Do I judge people by how others feel about them instead of by my true feelings?

Do I know how to help others?

Do I know how to ask for help when I need it?

Is it selfish to ask for help?

SS3831

WHAT IS THE POWER OF LOVE?

Read 1 Corinthians 13:1-13.

Things to think out:

Whom do I love?

Why do I love them?

Whom can't I love?

Is there a way to love those I can't seem to like?

WHAT IS THE POWER OF LOVE?

Read 1 Corinthians 13:1-13.

Things to think out:

Whom do I love?

Why do I love them?

Whom can't I love?

Is there a way to love those I can't seem to like?

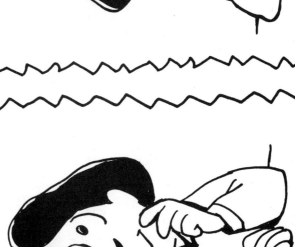

WHAT IS THE POWER OF LOVE?

Read 1 Corinthians 13:1-13.

Things to think out:

Whom do I love?

Why do I love them?

Whom can't I love?

Is there a way to love those I can't seem to like?

SS3831

IS THIS MY JOB?

Read Mark 16:14-18.

Things to think out:

Does Jesus expect me to tell others about His life, death, and resurrection?

Do I have the courage to tell others about Him? Am I afraid of being laughed at?

Is my everyday life a witness for Jesus?

IS THIS MY JOB?

Read Mark 16:14-18.

Things to think out:

Does Jesus expect me to tell others about His life, death, and resurrection?

Do I have the courage to tell others about Him? Am I afraid of being laughed at?

Is my everyday life a witness for Jesus?

IS THIS MY JOB?

Read Mark 16:14-18.

Things to think out:

Does Jesus expect me to tell others about His life, death, and resurrection?

Do I have the courage to tell others about Him? Am I afraid of being laughed at?

Is my everyday life a witness for Jesus?

SS3831

THANKS-A-GRAM

Make copies of the Thanks-a-Grams on page 20. Give each student at least three copies. Point out to your junior highers that we often forget to thank people. Some people don't realize they are valued because no one ever tells them so. This is a chance to give someone a pat on the back and to receive one. Students should watch the people around them, and when they see someone do something nice or helpful, they can jot down the good deed and give it to the person they wish to thank. Challenge your group to really think about how others help them and to notice people helping others. The Thanks-a-Grams will show the recipients that their acts of kindness do not go unnoticed. Try to avoid making this a contest.

Write the name of the recipient of the Thanks-a-Gram at the top. Make sure each student signs his own name. Encourage each student to write a personal note on the Thanks-a-Gram, maybe even including a Bible verse. Each should be delivered personally whenever possible.

Thanks-a-Grams may be copied on official-looking yellow paper. Introduce the project by showing or reading a telegram. You might want to create a telegraph office (a place with extra forms and pencils) so kids have a place to fill in their Thanks-a-Grams.

SS3831

THANKS — THANKS — THANKS — THANKS — THANKS — THANKS — THANK

THANKS-A-GRAM

THANKS — THANKS — THANKS

To: ______________________________

____

____

____

From: ______________________________

THANKS — THANKS — THANKS — THANKS — THANKS — THANKS — THANKS

THANKS — THANKS — THANKS — THANKS — THANKS — THANKS — THANKS

THANKS-A-GRAM

THANKS — THANKS — THANKS

To: ______________________________

____

____

____

From: ______________________________

THANKS — THANKS — THANKS — THANKS — THANKS — THANKS — THANKS —

THANKS — THANKS — THANKS — THANKS — THANKS — THANKS — THANKS —

THANKS-A-GRAM

THANKS — THANKS — THANKS

To: ______________________________

____

____

____

From: ______________________________

THANKS — THANKS — THANKS — THANKS — THANKS — THANKS — THANKS —

DISCUSSIONS

GETTING THE TALK FLOWING

The first thing to remember about getting junior highers into a discussion is that often they are perfectly willing to let you do all the discussing. The second thing to remember is that they will almost certainly ask questions for which you do not have answers. Be honest at all times without being judgmental. They will respect you if you admit you don't know an answer; they may not be forgiving if they catch you faking it! Try for a light touch instead of an intense discussion. Humor always breaks the ice as long as it isn't at anyone's expense.

Five discussion sheets follow. The first three work best if undertaken with small groups. The last two work best with large groups.

The purpose of "Why I Like Me; Why I Don't," page 23, isn't to seek flaws but to discover strengths. Make this clear to your students before you hand out the work sheet. Give them a little time to answer the questions; then ask them which question was most difficult or easiest to answer. Go with the flow instead of starting at the top of the page and working down. You don't need to cover all the questions, but allow plenty of time for them to talk about the things they like about themselves.

If a junior higher says she hates something about her body or personality, don't make light of it or deny it. Find out if others feel the same way about themselves. Get the whole group involved in helping each other make a change in their lives. Note: Dieting seems to be a big thing on the minds of junior highers who, in some cases, are still having a problem with baby fat. They are impatient to have well-developed figures. This sometimes results in eating disorders. Discuss the importance of good nutrition and the dangers of poor eating habits and dieting.

The purpose of "My Story," page 24, is to help junior highers consider what they think about themselves. In many ways "My Story" is similar to "Why I Like Me; Why I Don't," but it is done more anonymously and is more concerned with relationships with others. Have them complete their stories as honestly as they can. They need not put their names on the papers. Collect the papers, and look quickly through the sheets. Try to pick out humorous answers as well as serious ones to discuss. Don't be shocked or ignore any answers. Instead, try to discover why the answers were given.

After explaining that service to God can mean different things to different people, hand out copies of "Can I Serve God in This World?," page 25, and give students time to answer the questions. Then start at the top and ask for volunteers to share their answers. If they are slow to respond, be prepared with answers of your own that may not agree with theirs. Challenging their perceptions will help to get them talking. Junior highers enjoy talking about service to God, but they are sometimes afraid to actually do it because they feel conspicuous. A discussion will allow them to share their uncertainties and develop more courage to live as Christians.

                                                                                  SS3831

"Challenge Questions," page 26, is the toughest discussion for adults, but the one your group will probably like best. Junior highers want to talk about these things with adults, and they want to know that other kids feel as uncertain about these things as they do. If these questions make you uncomfortable, before undertaking this discussion, talk with your minister or a professional counselor. You may want to invite your minister or a counselor to join or even lead the discussion. Be honest if you don't know an answer, and avoid being judgmental. It may ease your students' level of discomfort if only a few "Challenge Question" sheets are handed out and they must share. You need not discuss every question. Someone may ask a question you feel unprepared to answer. For example, if the question deals with substance abuse, remind them that the Bible encourages moderation in all things. You may need to admit that you have difficulty with some topics before getting into the discussion. If you know you can't discuss a question in a reasonable manner, tell your students so and don't discuss it. Suggest someone else they could talk to about it or call on someone else to lead that part of the discussion.

Keep the only copy of "Faith Questions," page 27, or hand out copies to everyone. Suggest ahead of time to your adult helpers that you'd like them to get as involved in the discussion as the junior highers. "Faith Questions" may be used as a vehicle to prompt other activities, such as a prayer writing contest or a select-a-topic contest to decide on the theme for the "Create-a-Service" project. Make sure you know what your church teaches about the questions in "Faith Questions." It's even better if you can compare what other faiths believe without being judgmental.

SS3831

WHY I LIKE ME; WHY I DON'T

"Do you not know that your body is a temple of the Holy Spirit, who is in you, whom you have received from God? You are not your own; you were bought at a price. Therefore honor God with your body." 1 Corinthians 6:19-20

What does 1 Corinthians 6:19-20 mean to me?

When I look at my body, I don't like . . .

The things I like about my body are . . .

The things that give me problems about my attitudes and feelings are . . .

The best things about my personality are . . .

The things I'd most like to change about myself are . . .

The things about me that help me get along well with other people are . . .

The thing or person that often seems to get in the way of my being the person I want to be is . . .

The reason for this is . . .

Being a Christian helps me most when . . .

SS3831

MY STORY

My story began on _____, the day I was born in

_____. I am _____ years old now. What I like

most about this age is _____.

The thing I dislike most about this age is _____.

My family is made up of _____

_____. The

thing I like most about my family is _____.

The thing I like most about my home is _____.

My favorite relative is _____

because _____.

My best friend is _____, because

_____. He/she

likes me because _____.

My worst habit is _____. The thing I do best is

_____. Sometimes I am afraid when

_____. I like being with my church group

because_____. If I could be any animal, I would

be a _____ because _____.

If I could be someone else, I would be _____

because _____. If I ruled the world,

I would _____.

When I grow up, I want to _____. My faith in God is important

to me because _____.

SS3831

CAN I SERVE GOD IN THIS WORLD?

Serving God has always had its price. Early Christians were despised and sometimes fed to lions. In the Middle Ages a few people who claimed to be Christians held the power in Europe and kept other people in a form of slavery until the printing press made the Bible and other books available to all. In Nazi Germany, Jewish people and Christians who dared to say the Nazis were wrong were sent to concentration camps. One of these Christians was a man named Dietrich Bonhoeffer. Although he left Germany and came to the United States to tell about the atrocities, he returned to Germany and died in a concentration camp for his beliefs. In the 1950s a team of missionaries were killed by headhunters in South America. Today in Egypt Christians can be imprisoned for talking about Christ.

Most of us will never be faced with these kinds of challenges to our faith. Our greatest challenge may be trying to live as Christians when it isn't fashionable.

How can you serve God right now?

How can you serve God in your everyday life?

When others are making fun of someone or hurting someone, where can you get the courage to try to stop it?

Are you serving God when you try to be friends with someone who doesn't have many friends?

Why are some people so hard to like?

Have you ever considered a career in the ministry?

Who should be a religious leader?

How will you know which occupation is the right choice for you?

What do religious leaders do?

Finish the following sentences:

I can't feed all the hungry people in the world, but I can . . .

I can't like everyone equally, but I can . . .

I can't die on the cross for the sins of the world, but I can . . .

SS3831

CHALLENGE QUESTIONS

1. Do you have trouble getting along with one or both of your parents? Why do you think this is happening? How can you change things to make them better? Have you tried to look at things from your parents' point of view?

2. Imagine that you have a friend in school who is having trouble with his grades, mostly because he isn't studying. If he asks you to help him cheat on a test, will you do it? Why or why not? How can you refuse and still keep your friend? Are you really helping him if you help him cheat?

3. Imagine that you have a friend who takes drugs. What can you do about it? Should you try to do more? What?

4. Why are drinking alcohol and getting drunk considered cool by some kids? You are at a party having a lot of fun when someone arrives with alcohol or drugs. What do you do? How do you respond if it's offered to you?

5. Someone wants to be your friend. No matter how you look at this person, she is not the kind of friend you want. What do you do?

6. What do you do when you have sexual thoughts about someone? How can you control that feeling or need?

7. Your best friend is involved in a sexual relationship with someone. How do you feel about that? What do you say to your friend?

8. What questions do you have about sex?

9. How do you think God feels about sex?

10. Do you sometimes feel lonely and wonder if anyone else has ever felt as lonely as you?

 SS3831

FAITH QUESTIONS

Who is God?
- A. Creator of heaven and earth (Genesis 1:1)
- B. Jesus (John 14:10)
- C. Holy Spirit (Ephesians 2:22)

Has God ever spoken to you? How did He speak to you?

God has spoken to many people throughout the ages. He spoke to Moses from the burning bush and atop Mt. Sinai. He spoke to Paul on the road to Damascus. Does He speak to us in the same ways today?

Why do you pray?

Jesus not only told His disciples to pray, but taught them a sample prayer to follow. (Matthew 6:9-13) (This is a good time to decide if you want to have a prayer-writing contest for a morning prayer.)

Why do you go to church?

What special gifts does God give to people? Read 1 Corinthians 12:4-11.

Do you think people have these gifts today?
Which gift would you choose? Why?

Do you think you might have a spiritual gift you're not using?

Why do you believe in God?

Why is it sometimes embarrassing to talk about being a Christian?

With God's help, we can do any good thing. What does that mean to you?

SS3831

WORKING IT OUT TOGETHER

The purpose of this section is for junior highers to have a good time working together as they produce something worthwhile.

CREATE-A-SERVICE

This project may be used in your group meetings, at a gathering of several youth groups, or as a youth Sunday in your church. It takes time to organize and write, and your junior highers will need time to practice their parts. Discuss with the group what they want to include in their worship service. This will make the undertaking more their own. Let each student pick the part he wishes to help create. You may need extra adult help at this planning stage to work with small groups. Create-a-Service is a great way to help kids feel more a part of their church.

In general, these are some elements you might want to include:

1. Call to Worship or Invocation: Write a poem or responsive reading for the group to read alone or with the congregation. Come up with other ideas to create a welcome.

2. Scripture Reading: Select a Scripture passage and read it together or in parts, or act out a Bible story.

3. Music: Lead the singing of one or more hymns or choruses, or write new words to familiar tunes.

4. Thought for the Day: This should be a brief talk or personal testimony that one person gives. It may be read, acted out, made into a poem, mimed, or presented in some other creative way.

5. Prayer: Write a prayer and read it together, create a responsive prayer, or use a familiar prayer.

6. Collection: This may be a collection of a money offering, or you may decide to collect something else, such as slips of papers listing bad habits, good wishes for other people, or promises of what people will do to serve the Lord. Explain the collection to the congregation and hand out slips of paper on which they may write bad habits, good wishes, or promises to keep. During or after the service, you may want to burn the bad habits to symbolize giving them up. Make a collage of promises or good wishes to display in the church.

7. Benediction: Create words of parting that will be an inspiration for everyone in their walk with the Lord. An appropriate Scripture passage may best serve this purpose.

SS3831

SUGGESTIONS FOR WHEN THE MUSE FAILS

It's a good idea to have some inspirational books available, especially ones meant for teens. Your church library might have some old materials left from past years which your junior highers could use when searching for ideas.

Have a Bible concordance for students to use when they need to find verses on specific topics. Some much used topics are:

1 Corinthians 13:4-13 Love
Matthew 5:3-12 The Beatitudes
Matthew 5:13-16 Salt and Light
Psalm 121 God's Care for Us
Ecclesiastes 3:1-8 A Time for Everything

Familiar Prayers:

Day by day, dear Lord, of Thee three things I pray:
To see Thee more clearly, love Thee more dearly,
Follow Thee more nearly, day by day.
(13th century prayer of Richard, Bishop of Chichester)

Lord, make me an instrument of Thy peace.
Where there is hatred, let me sow love;
Where there is injury, pardon;
Where there is discord, union;
Where there is doubt, faith;
Where there is despair, hope;
Where there is darkness, light;
Where there is sadness, joy.
Grant that we may not so much seek to be consoled as to console;
To be understood as to understand;
To be loved as to love.
For it is in giving that we receive, it is in pardoning that we are pardoned; and it is in dying that we are born to eternal life.
(St. Francis of Assisi)

Also keep a selection of hymnals, chorus books, and contemporary Gospel music books available for junior highers to use when making music selections.

                                                                                    SS3831

CREATE-A-SKIT

Junior highers enjoy doing skits, but they also have a tendency to be shy or backward when in front of a group. Convince them that doing skits is just for fun. You know that it's also a good way to draw out the shy ones and provide gregarious kids with an outlet for their need to be on stage. There is no need for students to memorize their lines unless they really want to. You might explain to them that even professional actors sometimes use their own words as long as the meaning is the same as in the script. If students want to look at their scripts as they do their final performance, that's OK.

Skits are easiest to create if junior highers are divided into small groups with advisors. They do not necessarily have to make up the skits themselves. You might make a short skit available to each group; then let them do what they want with it. Or give each group the same skit and tell them to put their own spin on it. The public library has books of skits and short plays available. Of course, humorous skits are more fun than serious ones.

Skits may have biblical themes or everyday themes. Biblical skits usually cover familiar Bible stories such as:
> Noah and the ark
> The Prodigal Son
> Jesus feeding the five thousand

To make familiar stories more interesting, put them in a new perspective. Here are some ideas:
> A contemporary setting and "modern" language and situations
> Rhyming dialogue and narration
> Well-known songs or choruses (such as Noah singing "Row, Row, Row Your Boat")
> A modern news report of the event with interviews, weather report, sports, etc.

Another possibility of a more serious nature is to create skits around actual problems and challenges junior highers encounter in their lives. Some of these may turn out humorously and some may be intense.
> How to talk to a friend whose family is falling apart.
> How to deal with abusive parents.
> What to do for an alcoholic/drug-using friend.
> What to do with someone who is sad or depressed and talks about dying.
> How to make a friend.

CHRISTIANS ON TRIAL

The purpose of this activity is to help junior highers think about the evidence in their lives of their Christianity.

Each Christians on Trial enactment needs a judge, a defendant, a prosecuting attorney, and twelve jurors. You might also want an arresting officer. Everyone else is audience, and may be called on by the defendant in his defense if the defendant thinks that person can help prove his case. The defendant gets to be his own defense attorney. You'll want outgoing kids for the prosecuting attorney and judge. Try to choose a defendant with a sense of humor, since the defendant in the first enactment hasn't a clue about what is happening. The prosecuting attorney and judge have sheets of suggested questions and lines, but they may vary what they say if they do so with humor that's in good taste and is relevant.

Set up chairs to create a courtroom scene. Use an old choir robe for the judge's costume. Encourage students to add other props as they think of them. After the first group of participants are chosen, the judge and the prosecuting attorney may read their directions as the jury is seated and picks a foreman. The enactment begins with the arresting officer escorting the defendant to the bench. After the prosecuting attorney makes a summation, the jury should be allowed to adjourn for no more than ten minutes to make a decision, which the foreman will read aloud.

Explain that the purpose of this activity is to create a trial in which someone must supply evidence to prove he is a Christian. It's meant to be fun, but it's also serious. The defendant may not lie. Remind your group that being a Christian has been very dangerous in the past in some countries. The first Christians were persecuted. Christians who dared protest under the Nazis died in concentration camps. Chinese Christians were imprisoned when their country fell to communism. Many current missionaries are in danger from wars and local prejudices. The judge in this enactment may choose the country and time, and hand down his sentence accordingly.

After the first enactment, you may want to do another one immediately or choose volunteers for the next enactment. Let them have time to plan how they'll influence the verdict. The new judge may not pick the same sentence for the next defendant. No one should have copies of the prosecuting attorney's questions or the judge's choices. Any previous judge should be asked not to reveal the other choices he could have made.

PROSECUTING ATTORNEY QUESTIONS

Use any or all of these questions in any order you choose. The defendant must answer each one honestly. If you add questions of your own, use good taste and never be cruel.

What physical evidence is there in your home that you are a Christian? Does (item the person names) belong to you?

Is there any physical evidence in your room that you are a Christian?

Is there any physical evidence on your person that you are a Christian?

Have you ever in the past talked about Christ before witnesses? Are any of those witnesses present?

Do you attend church? How regularly? Can you prove that?

Do you attend youth group? Can you prove that?

If your church doesn't have a youth group that meets regularly, have you thought about doing something about that?

Why are you a Christian?

Have you ever successfully helped someone else become a Christian?

Summation:

Ladies and gentlemen of the jury, you have heard the evidence against (defendant's name). If you feel there is enough evidence in the life of (defendant's name) to find him/her guilty of the charge of being a Christian, I urge you to bring in a verdict of guilty. If there is not enough evidence, you have no choice but to find him/her not guilty.

JUDGE'S STATEMENTS

It is your job to keep the action going. You get to order the person brought to justice, recognize witnesses, and pick the time and country in which you will sentence the defendant. Follow your lines, as written, fairly closely to keep things moving.

(To the arresting officer) Please bring forward the prisoner.

(To prisoner) You, (defendant's name), have been charged with being a Christian. A jury has been selected to decide if that charge is true. You may ask me to call witnesses forward as you need them in your own defense. Please be seated.

(Prosecuting attorney takes over. Call him down if he gets too mouthy. After his summation you will say to the jury) You have heard the evidence. It is your job to decide if (defendant's name) is guilty or not guilty of being a Christian.

(When jury returns, ask) Mister/Madam Foreman, have you reached a decision?

(Upon hearing the verdict, choose the time and country and sentence the person accordingly.)

If defendant is found not guilty:
1. This is Lithuania in 1992. As you, (defendant's name), cannot prove you are a Christian, we can only suspect you of being a communist. You may go, but you will be watched. You are not eligible for any government position as we have seen what communism can do to our government.
2. This is present day America. You, (defendant's name), have not proved you are a Christian. You are free to go and live a lifetime of hopelessness without Christ.
3. This is China in 1991. You, (defendant's name), have not been found guilty of being a Christian, but the people you associate with here suggest you have tendencies to believe in God. You are free, but you will be watched.

If defendant is found guilty:
1. This is present day America. You, (defendant's name), have been found guilty of being a Christian. Go and live happily with the assurance that you have the love of God to sustain you in your times of joy and difficulty.
2. This is Rome one hundred years after the death of Christ. You, (defendant's name), have been found guilty of being a Christian. I sentence you to provide entertainment for the crowds as you are eaten by lions in the coliseum.
3. This is Germany in 1940. You, (defendant's name), have been found guilty of being a Christian. Do you swear to honor the Nazi flag, worship Adolf Hitler as a god, and ignore the murder of Jews, Gypsies, and protestors? (If defendant answers yes.) Then return to your home, but you will be watched. (If defendant answers no.) Then I sentence you to the concentration camps for attitude adjustment.

 SS3831

CRAFTS
BUMPER STICKERS

Materials: 2 pieces of clear adhesive plastic cut into 10" x 3" rectangles for each junior higher, 5 pieces of white paper cut 3/4" shorter and narrower than the clear adhesive plastic for each junior higher, colorful markers, pencils

Objective: To create an eye-catching, brief way to share a Christian message. Allow time for each student to make two bumper stickers. They may need four or five pieces of paper to allow for mistakes and start-overs.

Assembly: Draw a design and write a message on the paper rectangle. Carefully remove the backing from the clear adhesive plastic (saving the backing). Center your message on the adhesive plastic, facing the sticky surface. Replace the backing to protect the sticky border until you decide where to display the bumper sticker.

PAINTED TILES

Materials: 1 light-colored unglazed tile for each student (available at building supply stores); small cans of red, blue, white, black, brown, green, and yellow enamel paint; paint thinner; old rags; several paintbrushes; newspaper to protect table surfaces; pencils; patterns from a pattern book (available in craft stores); carbon paper; disposable plastic cups

Objective: To create an attractive trivet or wall hanging that symbolizes a biblical concept or truth without words. Help junior highers come up with appropriate symbols, such as butterfly–resurrection or new life, dove–Holy Spirit, hearts–love, tree or flowers–Christian growth, cross–Jesus' death, rainbow–God's promise, open Bible–God's Word.

Assembly: Draw a design on the tile or choose a pattern from the pattern book and trace it on the tile, using carbon paper. Paint the tile a variety of colors. Small amounts of paint may be mixed in disposable cups to create different colors. This project requires twenty-four hours to dry properly.

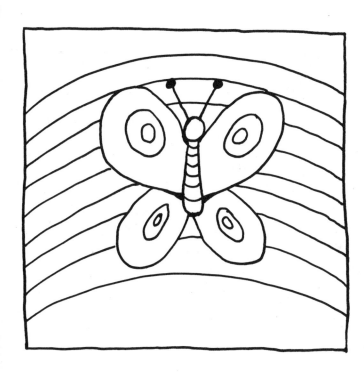

PUNCHED TIN LANTERN

Materials: A clean, empty can for each student (large fruit cans work well); hammers; 16-penny nails; pencils (for drawing original designs or tracing a simple pattern from a pattern book with carbon paper onto cans); a votive candle to put in each can; lots of newspaper; 6"-10" length of two-by-four boards; glossy black spray paint

Objective: To create punched tin art which will remind us that we can be lights to the world by serving others. Talk about how God wants His light to shine through us.

Assembly: Pack a can with newspaper rolled around a board so the can can't be easily crushed. Draw or trace a simple pattern on the can. Using a hammer and nail, punch holes approximately $1/4$" to $1/2$" apart along the lines of the design. Spray the can with black paint in a well-ventilated area. A candle may be attached to the inside of the can with drops of hot wax. The lantern should be placed on a fireproof surface where it won't be accidently knocked over when in use.

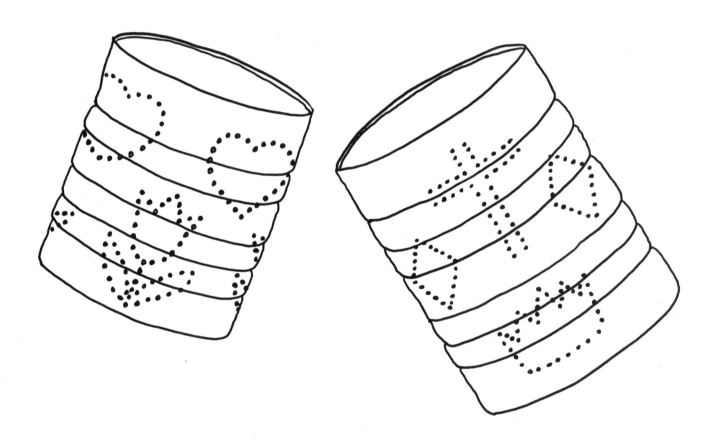

Hidden Word Plaque

Materials: 7" length of 1" x 2" board for each student, several lengths of $1/4$" square wooden dowels, craft saw, wood glue, clear spray varnish (optional), sandpaper, a copy of this page for each student

Objective: To create a hidden word plaque with a biblical message or thought.

Assembly: Decide which plaque you will make. Print your name on the back of a 7" piece of wood. Using this page for exact measurements, saw the required number of square dowel lengths needed for the plaque. Sand down any rough spots on the wood. Place the cut lengths of wooden dowel in place on the wooden background according to the pattern. Glue the lengths of dowel to the background. After the glue dries, spray the plaque with clear varnish.

(Actual size of square wooden dowels and plaques is shown.)

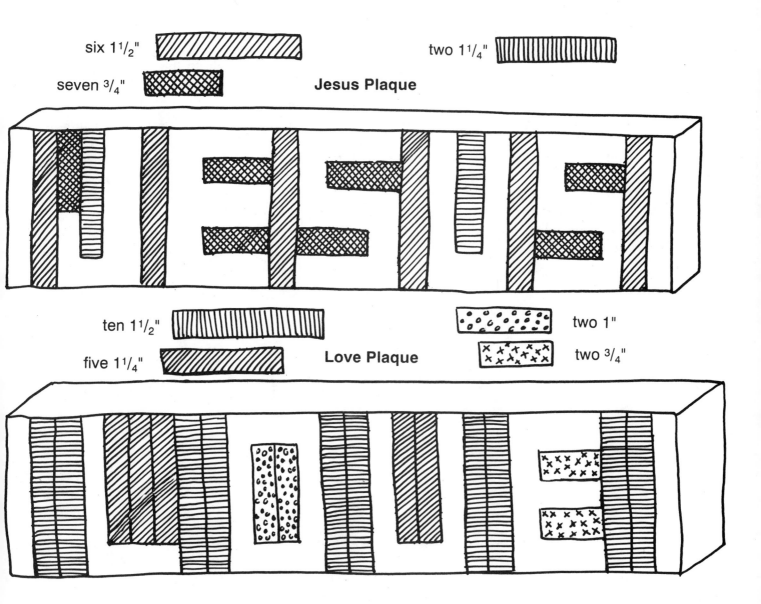

six $1^1/_2$"

seven $3/_4$"

two $1^1/_4$"

Jesus Plaque

ten $1^1/_2$"

five $1^1/_4$"

Love Plaque

two 1"

two $3/_4$"

SS3831

INDIAN BEADWORK BRACELET

Materials: 6" length of two-by-four board for each student, heavy-bladed knife, thumbtacks, short pencils, giant seed beads in various colors (they are easier to handle than smaller beads), thin needles, thin nylon thread, and thin metallic thread

Objective: To use an American Indian handicraft to make a bracelet that will serve as a witness of faith in God.

Assembly: To make a loom, stick a thumbtack in the center bottom of the board leaving a little space between the wood and the tack head. Cut 10 notches approximately $\frac{1}{8}$" apart on the upper edge at both ends of the board. Tie one end of the metallic thread to the thumbtack. Pull the thread up over the top of the board through the outside notches. Loop the thread around the thumbtack, reverse the direction, and pull the thread back across the top of the loom through the next set of notches. Continue laying the thread over the top of the board until all notches are filled. Reverse direction each time by looping the thread around the thumbtack. Do not overlap the threads. Tie the end of the metallic thread to the thumbtack. Then carefully insert a pencil diagonally under the threads and the loom is ready.

Thread a needle with about 40" of nylon thread. Tie a bead securely to the end of the thread, leaving a 3" tail of thread. Add 8 more beads to the thread. (Do not use any bead that is tight on the needle.) Lay the string of beads atop the loom threads approximately 1" from one end of the loom, each bead separated by a thread. Return the needle in the reverse direction through the beads beneath the metallic threads, and pull the nylon thread tight. Add 9 beads to the thread. Lay the beads across the loom threads beside the first row, a metallic thread between each bead. Return the needle through the beads beneath the loom threads, draw the nylon thread tight, and press the second row of beads tightly against the first row. Repeat until you have 4"-5" of beadwork, changing the bead colors to create different patterns. To complete the bracelet, remove the thumbtack and knot the loose threads as close to the weaving as possible at each end. Braid the loose threads before knotting the ends.

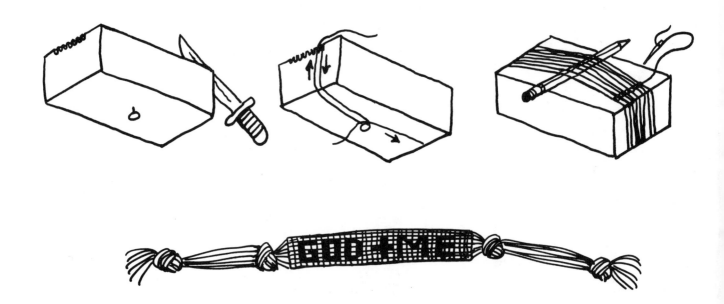

SS3831

BLUEBIRD HOUSE

Materials: This bluebird house may be made of scrap 1" thick lumber or a 6' board 1" x 8". The best woods for construction are white cedar, western cedar, cypress, or redwood. The wood does not need to be top grade, but knotholes will make the work more difficult. Do not use salt or chemically treated wood or wood with paint or varnish on it. You will also need rustproof nails or brass screws, a drill with $1\frac{1}{2}$" and $\frac{3}{8}$" bits, a hammer or screwdriver, and a saw (or a table saw and someone able to use it). You may be able to find someone in your church to cut the pieces of wood and drill the holes for you.

Objective: To create a nesting site for bluebirds, which are becoming a somewhat rare species. This project should also involve long-term care of the house to help this species survive.

The bluebird, sometimes called the blue robin, was once one of the most common songbirds. Modern farming methods have greatly reduced their numbers. Dead trees, which provide them with homes, are cut down. Fencerows, where they prefer to hunt grasshoppers, beetles, crickets, centipedes, and spiders, are kept mowed or are gone altogether. Bluebirds particularly enjoy hunting insects and living in orchards, but the spraying of the trees has contributed to their decline. They are frequently tormented by sparrows and starlings, which tend to invade their houses.

Talk about the importance of caring for God's creation.

Assembly: Follow the diagrams on page 40. The completed birdhouse will look like this.

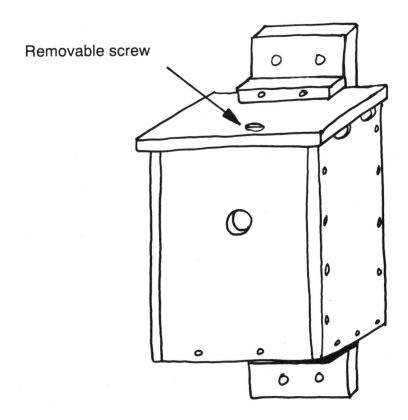

Removable screw

If using a 6' plank, cut the wood as shown (figure 1). If using scrap lumber, you will need the following pieces:

   top–8" wide x 9" deep
   back–6" wide x 20" long
   front–6" wide x 12" long with 1½" entry hole 9" from bottom edge
   two sides–7" deep with sides 12" at front and 13" at back, with vent holes at top edge
   bottom–6" wide x 5½" deep with four ³/₈" vent holes

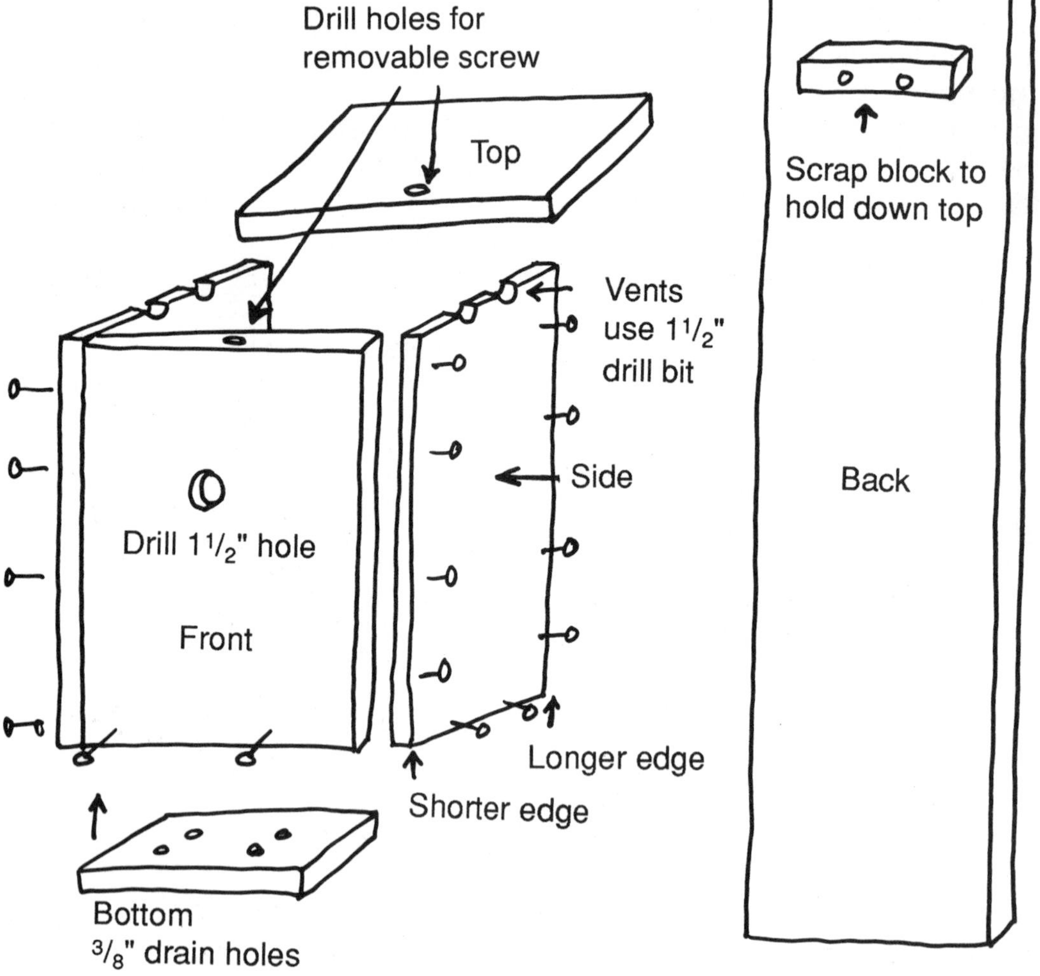

Drill holes for removable screw

Top

Drill 1½" hole

Front

Vents use 1½" drill bit

Side

Longer edge

Shorter edge

Bottom
³/₈" drain holes

Scrap block to hold down top

Back

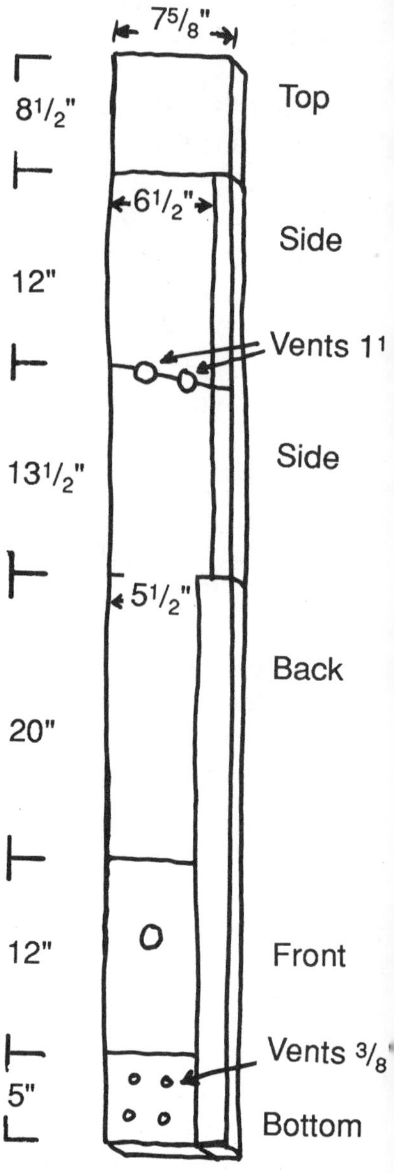

Top 8½"

Side 7⁵/₈"

6½"

12"

Vents 1¹

Side 13½"

5½"

Back 20"

12"

Front

5"

Vents ³/₈

Bottom

Figure 1

Ongoing Project Information: The location of the birdhouse is very important. Bluebirds are territorial, so their houses should be more than 100 yards apart in reasonably open areas with scattered trees, such as country cemeteries, golf courses, and pastures. The house should be mounted 4' to 20' above the ground on a post or tree. Keep in mind that it must be cleaned out, preferably shortly after the young bluebirds leave the nest. Pairs will sometimes begin a second nesting in the same year if their house is clean.

HARDENED CLAY ORNAMENTS AND BOWLS

This versatile clay can be air-hardened or baked solid in an oven.

    1 cup table salt
    1 cup cool, but not cold, water
    2 cups flour
    2 or 3 drops of food coloring (optional)

Mix salt and flour in a bowl. Add water a little at a time and knead on a lightly floured board until the mixture no longer sticks to your fingers. Store it in a tightly sealed container and keep it cool. Use it within a month if possible.

A wide variety of items may be made with this clay: mobiles of butterfly shapes, Christmas ornaments, fish symbol, and pendants and figurines created by pressing the clay into molds.

The clay becomes permanent when it's allowed to air-dry slowly. The air-dry method is suggested for creating figurines or other items of uneven thicknesses.

A quicker way to dry this clay after it is shaped is to bake it at 325 degrees for 1 hour, or until it's very firm. Less baking time is needed for thin pieces. To attach two pieces of clay together, moisten both surfaces with drops of water. Ornaments may be made by rolling the dough flat and cutting it with cookie cutters. Use a straw or pencil to punch holes in the ornaments for hangers or ribbon. When the clay is cool, paint it with poster paints or markers and glaze it with clear enamel spray paint.

This clay may also be used to make bowls and vases. Select a piece of ovenproof glass, such as a casserole dish or inexpensive flower vase. Thinly coat the outside of the vase or dish with cooking oil. Roll the clay 3/8" thick. Cover the vase or dish with the clay, trimming off the excess. Fancy shapes may be cut with cookie cutters and glued to the clay by moistening them with water. A rim for the vase or dish can be made by rolling ropes of clay and braiding or twisting them together. Secure this to the rim by moistening it with water. Bake, clay side up, and allow the clay to cool for several hours. Remove the casserole dish or vase. If food coloring was not added, the clay shape will be the color of baked bread. Spray it with clear or satin enamel to preserve it, or paint it with watercolors.

SS3831

PAPIER-MÂCHÉ PROJECTS

Materials: objects to cover (balloons, bottles, cans, etc.), torn strips or bits of newspaper, warm water, wallpaper paste or flour and water paste

Assembly: Soak bits or strips of newspaper in water until the paper is thoroughly saturated. Drain off the water and mix in paste. If you use flour and water paste, add a teaspoon of liquid bleach to the water to prevent mildew, especialy in humid climates. Layer the newspaper, overlapping the pieces over balloons, bottles, clean cans, or other objects. Allow each layer to dry somewhat before adding another. Ten layers is usually an adequate thickness for any project meant to have a hollow center.

Other Ideas: To create piñatas, cover balloons, dry completely, burst the balloons and paint the piñatas with poster paints or cover them with colorful bits of tissue paper dipped in paste. Piñatas may be sold as a fund-raising project, or you can just make them for fun. Make fancy boxes by covering cardboard boxes and lids with papier-mâché. Allow the papier-mâché to dry completely, paint the outside with poster paint or bright spray enamels, and line the inside with felt or corduroy. Make interesting vases by covering bottles or cans with papier-mâché and painting them when they're dry. Another interesting effect is to rub brown shoe polish on dry papier-mâché, then spray it with clear satin enamel to give it a wood-like look.

Create figurines or jewelry by soaking finely shredded paper in paste-water until it dissolves completely. Then squeeze out the water and mold the paper into shapes. When dry, paint the shapes. Make beads by shaping the mixture around pieces of wire. After the beads have dried, paint them and spray them with clear gloss enamel, and remove the wire.

CRAFT MATERIAL RECIPES

Many times you have an idea or see something you'd like your students to make, but the commercial materials are too expensive or aren't exactly what you want. The following recipes are relatively inexpensive and safe to use.

MURAL PAINT

$1\frac{1}{2}$ cups powdered laundry starch
1 quart boiling water
$1\frac{1}{2}$ cups soap flakes
$\frac{1}{2}$ tbsp. poster paint for each color desired

Mix the starch with enough cold water to make a paste. Add boiling water and cook (stirring constantly to prevent lumps) until the mixture is clear and glossy looking. Let the mixture cool a little, then add soap flakes, stirring until well mixed and smooth. Divide the mixture into 8-oz. glass jars and add a different poster color to each jar.

Use this paint for murals or pictures. Its major attribute is that it may be textured with fingers or other objects. It washes out of clothing somewhat better than most paints.

CORNSTARCH CLAY

6 tbsp. cornstarch
$\frac{3}{4}$ cup salt
$\frac{3}{4}$ cup boiling water

Mix the salt and cornstarch in a heavy pan. Pour boiling water over the mixture and stir it until it's smooth. Heat the mixture on the stove and stir it until it forms a soft ball in the middle of the pan. Knead it for ten minutes. Wrap it in waxed paper when it's cool enough to handle comfortably. Place it in a closed jar to keep the mixture moist until you are ready to use it. This clay will crack when allowed to air-dry.

PLAY-KLAY

2 cups flour
1 cup salt
4 tsp. cream of tartar
2 cups warm water
3 tbsp. salad oil
Food coloring
A few drops of oil—peppermint, wintergreen, or cloves for scent (optional)

Mix flour, salt, and cream of tartar well in a heavy pan. Add salad oil, warm water, a few drops of coloring, and scented oil (optional). Mix it thoroughly. Cook it over low heat, stirring constantly until a ball is formed and it is not sticky. Play-Klay may be reused many times. It does not dry into hardened shapes, but will keep for months in an airtight container in a cool place. Junior highers may wish to make this for their own use or as gifts for younger children.

Shining Star Publications, Copyright © 1994

SS3831

GAMES

During the ages immediately before and during the junior high years, the group is everything! The herding instinct is strong, and not fitting in with the group can be devastating. Team games and activities can build cooperation and encourage acceptance of one another. Watch for opportunities to give places of leadership to shy students and those less well accepted. Look for ways to help them shine and improve their "positions" in the group.

Try to get across to your junior highers, without being preachy, the importance of accepting one another because God made us the way we are for a reason, and He loves us all.

CHOOSING TEAMS

If you're looking for a new way to choose teams or partners for games, try these:

Have junior highers line up by birth dates with January at one end of a line and December at the other end. Split the group evenly by number with those born at the beginning of the year on one team and those born at the end of the year on the other team. To select partners, the first two at the beginning of the year are partners and so on through the year.

Have students do a blind lineup by height. Each one closes his eyes, then pats others on the top of the head to find where he fits by height. When they are lined up by height, divide the line evenly in two and pivot on the center so that the shortest person ends up facing the tallest. Divide this double line in half so that the shortest and tallest are on one team and the middle-sized kids are on the other. To select partners, stop where the lines are facing and let students choose the people they see in front of them.

Line up students by alphabetical order of first names from A to Z. If two have the same first name, the letters in their last name are used to determine order. Divide the line numerically in half for teams or pivot so that A becomes Z's partner.

NAME THAT CHARACTER

This Bible trivia game is based on Bible characters. Two to four junior highers can play, or you may want to divide your group into small teams to compete against one another. Give each person or team a Bible. Ask a Bible character trivia question and give the Bible reference. If students do not know the answer to the question, they may use their Bibles to find it. The first player to raise a hand gets to answer the question. If the answer is correct, that person or his team gets five points. If the answer is wrong, another player or member of another team may give an answer. If that player answers the question correctly, he or his team gets ten points! Each incorrect answer makes the correct answer worth five more points. If a question is answered incorrectly by three players or teams, the fourth player gets twenty points for answering it correctly!

1. Who had five smooth stones as his defense? 1 Samuel 17:40 (David)
2. Which disciple was a thief? John 12:4-6 (Judas)
3. Who was also called Paul? Acts 13:9 (Saul)
4. Which prophet condemned the idle rich? Amos 6:4 (Amos)
5. Who commanded Solomon's army? 1 Kings 4:4 (Benaiah)
6. Who was Jacob's father-in-law? Genesis 29:21-30 (Laban)
7. Who found a baby while she was bathing? Exodus 2:5-6 (Pharaoh's daughter)
8. Which disciple doubted Jesus' resurrection? John 20:24-25 (Thomas)
9. Which king of Israel had the shortest reign? 1 Kings 16:15 (Zimri)
10. What was the name of Jesus' friend who was buried in a cave? John 11:38-43 (Lazarus)
11. Who was the man who planted the first vineyard? Genesis 9:20 (Noah)
12. Whose wife told him to curse God? Job 2:9 (Job's)
13. Which disciple was brought to Jesus by his brother? John 1:40-42 (Simon Peter)
14. Which apostle was a Roman citizen? Acts 23:27 (Paul)
15. Whose sick mother-in-law did Jesus heal? Mark 1:30 (Simon's)
16. Which judge had seventy sons? Judges 8:29-35 (Gideon)
17. Who wrote over a thousand songs? 1 Kings 4:32 (Solomon)
18. Which disciple was sent to the island of Patmos? Revelation 1:9 (John)
19. What evil king ordered all infant boys in Bethlehem killed? Matthew 2:16 (Herod)
20. Which prophet was accompanied by a harpist? 2 Kings 3:14-16 (Elisha)
21. Which disciples were called the Sons of Thunder? Mark 3:17 (James and John)
22. Who shut the door of the ark? Genesis 7:16 (God)
23. Which disciple brought Peter to Jesus? John 1:41-42 (Andrew)
24. What king had seven older brothers? 1 Samuel 17:12-14 (David)
25. Who wore a camel hair tunic? Matthew 3:4 (John the Baptist)
26. What tax collector gave Jesus a banquet? Luke 5:29 (Levi)
27. Who was the first king of Israel? 1 Samuel 10:1 (Saul)
28. What was Jacob's other name? Genesis 32:28 (Israel)
29. Whom did God choose to lead the Israelites after Moses? Joshua 1:1-2, 6 (Joshua)
30. Who sent men to spy on Jesus? Luke 20:19-20 (Teachers of the Law and chief priests)

SS3831

BIBLE SAFARI

To play this game, each team member needs a Bible. The object of the game is to find each animal listed below in Scripture, list the reference, and mark the page in the Bible with a bookmark. The first team to find all the animals or the team who has found the most animals when the time is up wins the game.

1. leopard _____

2. lion _____

3. lamb _____

4. locust _____

5. frogs _____

6. fish _____

7. cow _____

8. ewe _____

9. wolf _____

10. dove _____

11. raven _____

12. spider _____

13. snail _____

14. eagle _____

15. horses _____

SS3831

BIBLE CHARADES

Divide the group into two teams. Copy the list of Bible stories below, cut them apart, and put them in a bag or box. The teams take turns acting out the Bible stories. A member of one team picks a Bible story slip and has sixty seconds to act it out, without speaking, while his team members try to guess it. If his team guesses the story in the allotted time, they get ten points. If they cannot guess it, the other team may guess. If the other team guesses correctly, they get fifteen points. The game continues until one team has fifty points.

BIBLE STORIES

Delilah cuts Samson's hair

Jesus walks on water

Eve eats the forbidden fruit

Joseph's brothers sell him

Moses parts the Red Sea

John baptizes Jesus

Daniel in the lions' den

The Prodigal Son returns home

Jesus is born

Moses receives the Ten Commandments

Queen Esther saves her people

Joseph receives a coat of many colors

Rebekah helps Abraham's servant and his camels at the well

Noah builds an ark

Jesus heals a blind man

Cain kills Abel

Joshua and the defeat of Jericho

Moses sees a burning bush

Jesus feeds five thousand

Jonah in the whale

The Good Samaritan

Jesus calms a storm

David kills Goliath

Noah on the ark during the flood

The Last Supper

Jesus chooses disciples

Zacchaeus climbs a tree to see Jesus

SS3831

CAMCORDER CAPERS

If they do it, you will record it.

OUR VERY OWN PLAY

Select a skit or play, possibly a melodrama. Generally, comedy works best. Have the props they will need on hand. Visit a rummage sale or resale shop for old clothing for costumes. Read through the play a few times, then do it. Record the play with a camcorder. Laughing together is the objective of this activity, so students needn't memorize their lines.

HISTORY HERITAGE

This is a special project aimed at preserving your church's heritage. Some of your church's older members may have been involved in starting and building the church. Interview them on tape. Ask them to share their special memories of the church in years past. Consult local history books for questions students might ask. Use early photographs of the church and its activities too. Later you and your students may wish to edit the tapes to create a professional looking work with multiple copies that will be a valuable part of your church library.

MUSICAL VIDEOS

Allow junior highers to select their favorite contemporary Christian songs and choruses to create their own music videos. Or challenge them to write their own songs. Students may perform the songs together and in solos or duets. Or they may involve the music department of your church. Encourage creativity. Sell the videos to other junior highers.

COMMERCIALS

1. Let your students do take-offs on popular commercials and videotape them.
2. Let them make commercials selling different aspects of religion to other young people. These may be of interest to your local radio or television station for fillers at Christmas or Easter.
3. Let them make commercials selling each other as the perfect best friend.

VIDEOTAPE IDEAS

Now that your students know how to videotape, what's the next step?
1. Create a videotape library for your church.
2. Have a videotape party. Serve popcorn, soda, and laughter.
3. If you have a really good tape that a wider audience would enjoy, see if you can get it played on public access TV.
4. Have a family night, inviting all your students' families for dinner and a movie.

SS3831

SCAVENGER HUNTS

STAR OF DAVID SEARCH

Depending on the size of your group, make approximately ten stars for each student. Choose a large room with many pieces of furniture. Tape stars in place with two-sided tape or curls of tape before your junior highers arrive. Some stars should be in plain sight and others hidden, but not inside anything that must be opened. Students may get down on their knees or even lie down to look on the bottoms of chairs, etc., but they may not move anything or open anything. You may wish to have small prizes for those who find the most stars, or have a grab bag of prizes and let students, starting with the winners, choose what they want.

Cut two of poster board and glue together to make star template.

"PRETTY AS A PICTURE" HUNT

For this scavenger hunt, divide into teams of five to ten students. Each team will need a list of pictures to be taken, an instant camera, a roll of 12 exposure film, a car or van large enough to hold the entire team, and an adult driver. The challenge is to take ten pictures that contain the subject matter on the list with at least one member of the group in each picture. Every person in the group must be in at least one of the ten photographs. Make a list of picture requirements to fit your local circumstances. Here are some suggestions:

- A local celebrity (You may specify or allow students to define a celebrity.)
- Sled riding, fishing, or some other seasonal activity
- A law officer
- A church entrance
- A bridge sign
- Someone eating at a fast-food restaurant
- Someone trying on shoes (or something else you specify) in a store
- A fire fighter
- A city population sign
- A local landmark

When approaching a specific person, students should explain that they are on a scavenger hunt. There needn't be winners of the hunt since the fun is in doing it, but the team which returns first with ten recognizable photographs may be called the winner.

SS3831

TALENT SHOWS

THE DO-IT-YOURSELF TALENT SHOW

Challenge each student to come to the next meeting with something to perform. (The only limitations should be that stunts can't be dangerous.) Let students work in pairs or small groups if they prefer. A list of possible acts is offered below. If at all possible, videotape the show and later have a popcorn and video party.

CHURCH FAMILY SHOW

What do you do in dreary weather? Have your junior highers organize a talent show involving everyone in the church as acts or audience. Encourage people of all ages and whole families to display their talent or humor. Your students can sign up acts, do publicity, act as ushers, design a program and print it, sell popcorn and soft drinks, emcee the show, and provide short skits between the acts. Be sure to videotape the program for later viewing.

TAKE THE SHOW ON THE ROAD

Perhaps you can arrange with a mall or local shopping area to entertain shoppers. Your group might be the whole show, or they might invite shoppers to join in the fun. You may want to put on the show for a worthy cause, such as flood relief, a food kitchen, or missions. Have offering buckets in which people may put their donations. Ask a student to share his or her Christian testimony or a short Bible devotional at the end of the program.

It's possible, with advance publicity, that shoppers could come prepared to be part of the show. For a small charge your group can make videotapes of their acts.

TALENT SHOW ACTS

singing
playing an instrument
miming a song
skits
stand-up comedy
doing a dramatic Bible reading
miming a Bible story
clowning
reading poetry
drawing something
craft demonstration
reading a funny story
stupid pet tricks
home video stunts

UNTIE THE KNOT

Students clump together as tightly as possible, each grabbing someone's hand (not both hands of the same person). The object is to work together to untie the knot without letting go of hands. They may find themselves in a single large circle, a couple of interlocked circles, or still hopelessly scrambled if teamwork fails.

INVERT THE CHAIN

Choose two teams of equal number, as many as twenty people to a team. Players stand in line behind each other. Each player reaches back between his legs with his left hand to grasp the right hand of the person behind him and forward with his right hand to grasp the left hand of the person in front of him. The last player in the line lies down, still clasping hands. The person in front of him walks backward, straddling behind him until the entire line is lying down with hands still linked. When the last team member's head touches the ground, the chain is inverted. Players may reverse the chain again and resume their original standing positions without breaking their handclasps.

BEWARE THE "THING"

After setting boundaries to the playing field, select two people as "It." With a right and left hand clasped, their objective is to wrap around other players, thus making them part of the "Thing." Each captured player is added to the "Thing" chain, any part of which can capture other players. The objective is to get the captured players working together to capture all the free players.

TEAMWORK

Students break up into pairs and compete in games such as wheelbarrow or three-legged races. The point of these activities is to work together. Pairs line up on one side and race to a finish line. The first team to cross the finish line wins.

 SS3831

BRAIN TEASERS

SEE AND SAY

In each example find the Christian saying by looking at the position of one word in relation to the other, the shape of the word, or the picture.

1. Example: **ABLE** **ABLE** parables	2. VICTORY WORLD	3. BABEL
4. RUBY C	5. JESUS PILATE	6. S T 1 P I R I
7. COVENANT	8.	9. DEATH LIFE
10. STAND I	11.	12. JONAH BOARD
13. T S LIFE P I R I	14.	15. JERICHO

SS3831

NUMBERS WITH MEANING

Certain numbers in the Bible are believed to represent certain ideas. For example: 3 is the number of God, 4 is the number of the created world, 7 implies fullness or completeness, 12 is for the people of God, 40 implies change. When you look up the numbers to complete this activity, notice how these numbers seem to explain things.

1. Genesis 2:2   To complete Creation and rest, God took _____ days.

2. Genesis 7:12   Noah saw it rain for _____ days.

3. Genesis 18:32   Abraham convinced God to save Sodom if this many righteous were found _____ people

4. Genesis 29:20, 27   To marry Rachel, the woman he loved, Jacob worked two terms equaling _____ years.

5. Exodus 7:19; 8:2, 16, 21; 9:3, 9, 18; 10:4, 21; 11:5   To convince Pharaoh of His power, God struck Egypt with _____ plagues.

6. Exodus 20:3-17   To guide His people, God provided _____ commandments.

7. Numbers 32:13   Moses was forty when he left Egypt. Forty years later he returned. He died after leading the Israelites in the desert for _____ years.

8. Joshua 6:4   The walls of Jericho fell down after Joshua marched his army around them for _____ days.

9. 1 Samuel 3:8   The Lord called the boy Samuel _____ times.

10. 1 Samuel 17:16   Goliath challenged the Israelites to send out a champion _____ times.

11. 1 Kings 18:31   Elijah built an altar of this many stones to represent Israel's _____ tribes.

12. 1 Kings 18:34   Elijah soaked his sacrifice and the altar with water _____ times.

Total of numbers from first page _____

SS3831

13. Job 42:13   After he was tested by all kinds of misery, Job was blessed with _____ children.

14. Matthew 2:11   The wise men gave Baby Jesus _____ gifts.

15. Matthew 4:2   After His baptism, Jesus fasted for _____ days.

16. Matthew 18:22   Jesus told Peter to forgive seventy- _____ times.

17. Matthew 27:63   Jesus promised to rise from the dead after _____ days.

18. Mark 14:41   In Gethsemane, Jesus woke up His sleeping disciples _____ times.

19. Luke 6:13-16   Jesus chose this many men to be His close followers. _____ disciples

20. John 11:17   Jesus bought Lazarus back to life after he was in his tomb for _____ days.

21. John 13:38   Jesus warned Peter he would deny Him _____ times.

22. Acts 6:2-3   Needing men to care for the sick and the poor, an additional seven men were chosen to help the _____ disciples.

23. Philemon is actually addressed to (how many) _____ people.

24. Revelation 1:4   In this book, John wrote to _____ churches.

25. Revelation 13:18   John gave this number as the mark of the beast in the end times.

_____

Total of numbers from this page

_____

Total of numbers from page 53

_____

If your numbers are correct, total them to find out the age of the man who lived the longest, Methuselah. Check Genesis 5:27.

_____

LET'S EAT

ACROSS

1. Matthew 23:24   A hypocrite worries about swallowing gnats and swallows a ___ instead.
4. Exodus 3:8   The new home of the Israelites was a land flowing with ___ and honey.
5. Genesis 18:8 Tender calf, ___, and milk were Abraham's idea of angel food.
7. Luke 6:1   Jesus' disciples ate ___ in the fields.
9. Psalm 69:21   ___ sounds like a terrible thing to give a person who is thirsty.
10. Genesis 24:17   Rebecca gave ___ to Abraham's servant.
11. Numbers 13:23   The men sent to explore Canaan gathered grapes, ___, and figs.
14. Jeremiah 24:1   Jeremiah's vision from God was two baskets of ___.
17. Mark 1:6   John the Baptist dined on ___ and wild honey.
18. Luke 15:23   The Prodigal Son's father forgave his wild-living son and ordered a feast for him of fattened ___.
19. Luke 24:30   When Jesus broke ___, His two followers finally recognized Him.

DOWN

1. Numbers 11:5   The children of Israel thought manna was boring. They wanted ___ with their leeks and onions.
2. Mark 15:23   On the cross Jesus was offered wine mixed with ___.
3. Deuteronomy 24:20   God told His people to leave their second crop of ___ for widows, orphans, and aliens.
4. Numbers 11:5   The Israelites also wanted ___ with their leeks and onions.
6. 1 Kings 17:4   God sent ___ to feed Elijah.
7. Numbers 13:23   The land God gave the Israelites was so fertile, it took two men to carry one bunch of ___.
8. Daniel 4:33   Nebuchadnezzar's pride brought him so low he ended up dining on ___.
10. John 2:9   At a wedding feast Jesus turned water into ___.
12. Exodus 16:31   ___ was white as coriander seed and tasted of honey.
13. Numbers 11:5   The Israelites wanted ___ with their leeks and onions too.
14. Matthew 14:17   Jesus fed the population of a small town with just two ___ and a few loaves of bread.
15. Psalm 69:21   Because ___ is bitter, it doesn't sound like it would improve the flavor of food.
16. Psalm 19:10   ___ is good to eat, for it is sweet.

SS3831

WATER, WATER, EVERYWHERE

Life cannot exist without water. Water is frequently referred to in the Bible. Not only is it used to ease thirst, but it has many other purposes. Jesus and Peter walked on water, although Peter's faith faltered and he sank. Water in the Bible is used for washing away not only dirt, but also sickness, pride, guilt, and sins. Below are some significant examples of water and its use.

1. Water is so important, God created it on the _____ day of creation. (Genesis 1:1-5)

2. When God's creatures became too violent for Him to bear, He washed them all away with _____. (Genesis 6:17)

3. When a murder couldn't be solved in ancient times, the elders of the town nearest the victim's body escaped responsibility for not finding the murderer by washing their hands over the body of a sacrificed _____. (Deuteronomy 21:6)

4. Naaman, the commander of the King of Aram's army, wanted to be cured of his leprosy, but he was furious when Elisha suggested that he _____ seven times in the waters of the insignificant Jordan River. (2 Kings 5:10)

5. When a mob cried for the execution of Jesus, Pilate rejected his responsibility in the death by washing his _____. (Matthew 27:24)

6. Jesus cured a man's blindness by sending him to wash mud from his eyes in the _____. (John 9:7)

7. To make His disciples understand the idea of service to others, Jesus performed the act of a servant by washing their _____. (John 13:5)

8. Paul was forgiven for persecuting early followers of Christ; then God told him to be baptized and have his _____ washed away. (Acts 22:16)

SS3831

"BRAIN TEASERS" ANSWER KEY

SEE AND SAY, page 52

1. Parables
2. Victory over the world
3. Tower of Babel
4. Red Sea
5. Jesus before Pilate
6. One in the Spirit
7. Ark of the covenant
8. Walk on water
9. Life after death
10. I understand
11. Light of the World
12. Jonah overboard
13. Life in the Spirit
14. Holy Bible
15. Fall of Jericho

NUMBERS WITH MEANING, page 53

1. 7	6. 10	11. 12	16. 7	21. 3
2. 40	7. 40	12. 3	17. 3	22. 12
3. 10	8. 7	13. 10	18. 3	23. 3
4. 14	9. 3	14. 3	19. 12	24. 7
5. 10	10. 40	15. 40	20. 4	25. 666

Methuselah died at 969 years.

SS3831

LET'S EAT, page 55

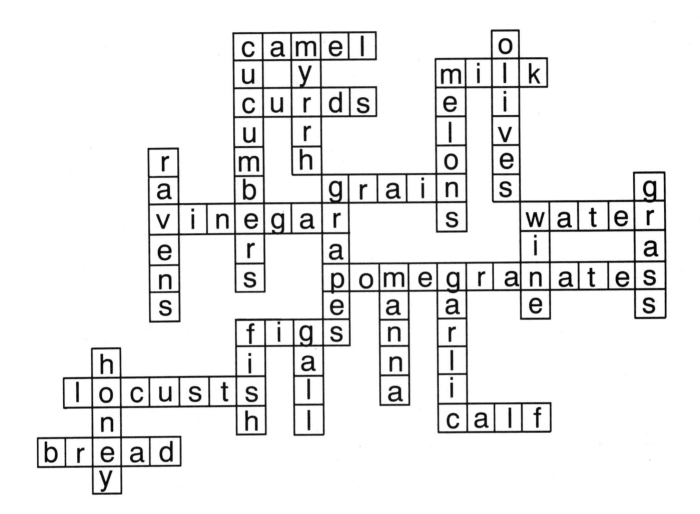

WATER, WATER, EVERYWHERE, page 57

1. first
2. floodwaters
3. heifer
4. wash
5. hands
6. Pool of Siloam
7. feet
8. sins

SS3831

STEWARDSHIP

GOOD AND FAITHFUL SERVANTS

"In the beginning God created the heavens and the earth. So God created man in his own image, . . . male and female he created them. God blessed them and said to them, 'Be fruitful and increase in number; fill the earth and subdue it. Rule over the fish of the sea and the birds of the air and over every living creature that moves on the ground.'" Genesis 1:1, 27-28

As the successors of Adam and Eve, we have inherited the earth. We have fulfilled God's command to multiply and fill all the earth. In some places we have done too well, overpopulating the earth until it can barely support life—human, plant, or animal. We have subdued, and in some cases driven to extinction, the creatures of the earth. Now we must do what we can to preserve those that remain, while maintaining a responsible way of living. As God's servants on earth, we should do the best we can by our world and make it a better place for tomorrow.

The following suggestions are thoughts or projects which will encourage junior highers to be more responsible for their world.

ADOPT A PIECE OF EARTH IN NEED OF TLC

Some states have an official adopt-a-highway project that you might wish to join, or choose a section of road in your community and take responsibility for keeping litter picked up there. Find a city lot to clean and clear and, with the owner's permission, use it as a garden or play area. In some areas, public parks or access areas need tending, but there are no funds available to pay to have the work done. Some country cemeteries are desperately in need of care. Get permission for your cleanup efforts from those responsible for the area. Notify the appropriate law enforcement agency if you are working along a road.

Wherever you work, put up a sign for everyone to see: We're taking care of God's creation.

TRY RECYCLING

Does your church have a recycling program? If not, start one. Set up recycle boxes and be responsible for taking the materials to a recycling station. Collect used bulletins, paper from the office, and aluminum and plastics from the kitchen. Accept responsibility for your family's recycling program, or do your own recycling if no one in the family is doing it.

LEARN MORE ABOUT GOD'S CREATIONS

Invite local experts on animals, bats, birds, reptiles, plants, rocks, or astronomy to talk to your group. Ask them to bring samples for kids to look at. Plan a field trip to a farm, wildlife area, museum, planetarium, working mine, cave, or highway project through interesting rock strata. Before or during the event, talk about God's creation. Look up meaningful Bible passages, such as Psalm 104, to read and discuss together.

BE INFORMED CONSUMERS

Responsibility for the earth also means buying responsibly. Buy things which use minimal packaging. If possible, buy things in recyclable packaging. Buy things that are the least harmful to the environment, such as a pump-action sprayer instead of an aerosol can. Use scented candles or potpourris instead of spray or solid air fresheners. Instead of using powerful drain openers and cleaners, use wire "snakes" and plungers. Buy things which are well-made instead of cheap junk that will quickly add to the waste sent to landfills.

Discuss other ways junior highers can be responsible before God in their everyday choices.

SS3831

CONSIDER LIFE-STYLES

If a home can be cooled by opening the windows, why not do that instead of using an energy-consuming air conditioner? Opening windows during cool summer nights and closing windows and curtains during the day can sometimes keep a home cool all day. Open blinds and curtains on sunny winter days to allow solar warming to the home. Clean out drains weekly with boiling water to eliminate the need for caustic drain openers. If a drain begins to slow, pour in 1/2 cup baking soda and 2 ozs. vinegar, allow it to fizz, and follow it with boiling water. Use sponges and washable rags instead of paper towels. Use a handkerchief instead of tissues. If you don't think you can eat it, don't take it. Use leftover food in creative dishes. Huge amounts of food are wasted in this country each year. If you break it, try fixing it instead of throwing it away and buying a new one. If clothing or toys or other items aren't worn out, don't throw them away. Give them to a charitable group who will share them with those who are less fortunate.

After Jesus fed 5000 people, He had His disciples gather the leftovers. "Let nothing be wasted." He said. That should be our attitude all the time.

PLANT SOMETHING

Consider planting a tree or a garden of flowers or vegetables. Is there an area around your church that your youth group could plant and cultivate? Consider growing vegetables and fruit to give to the poor or to sell at a country market to make money to give the church or to the poor. Grow flowers to beautify the church, for the enjoyment of the members. Plant a tree as a long-term commitment to improved air quality.

SHARE TALENTS

God wants us to share the gifts He has given us with others. Do you have musical talent that you could share in church? Do you have artistic talents that could be used to beautify the church, your home, or your community? Are you good at sports? You can help teach physical skills to younger children or help those with limitations get some exercise. Use your brain to think of ways to help others. Do you have the gift of empathy? Be a friend, allowing others to confide in you.

TRULY ACCEPT RESPONSIBILITY

Take responsibility for keeping your room neat and clean. Help around the house without complaining. To do so builds character. Earn money for your own donations to the church, because giving from the heart pleases God.

Talk about how responsible Christians influence others for the Lord. Read and discuss 1 Timothy 4:12.

CARING ABOUT PEOPLE TOO

As you and your group spend time with one another, you tend to begin taking one another for granted. No two of you have the same talents, the same appearance, the same abilities, or the same desires. Pass out slips of paper to each person in the group (including yourself) so that each student has enough paper to write a short note to each of the others. Seat the group in a large circle so that no one can read what anyone else writes. Ask each to begin by writing what he appreciates about the person on his right. The brief note may begin "I like you because . . ." or "The thing I like most about you is . . . " Each student should find something good to say about each person in the group. Encourage them to mention important things like attitude and actions, not things like looks or clothes. When everyone is done, pass the notes to the appropriate people. The notes may be read silently or taken home to read later. Discuss the importance of looking for something good in everyone. Encourage students to begin telling others, especially family members, why they care about them.

BUILDING A BETTER BODY

"Do you not know that your body is a temple of the Holy Spirit, who is in you, whom you have received from God? You are not your own; you were bought at a price. Therefore honor God with your body." (1 Corinthians 6:19-20)

Few of us are entirely pleased with our bodies, but we can take care of them so that they not only last longer but will better serve God. Try thinking of your body as a finely tuned machine requiring constant care and attention.

If we lie around and don't get proper exercise, our joints weaken and our muscles grow flabby. If we eat junk instead of healthy food, our systems tend to back up and leave excess calories which plump up our fat cells. If we don't bathe frequently, our "finish" gets grimy. If we don't rest properly, our brain system gets cranky and the entire machine wears out more quickly. If our brain system is fed a steady diet of violent movies, foul language, and obscene pictures, the process becomes a perfect example of garbage in, garbage out.

MAINTENANCE AGREEMENT

I agree to tend and maintain the earthly body God has purchased for me through the death of His Son until it is exchanged for the model granted me by eternal life.

1. I agree to fuel it properly, but not to excess, with heathy food instead of junk food and fad diets that could lead to a system breakdown.
2. I agree to keep it bathed and wear clean clothing to keep the "finish" gleaming and attractive.
3. I agree to use it well, exercising its many joints and muscles to keep them in fit running condition.
4. I agree to rest it properly to prevent excessive wear to parts and damage to the brain system.
5. I agree to carefully select the information entered into my brain system so that valuable storage space isn't taken up with violent images, bad language and thoughts, and wasteful anger.

By accepting my body as a temple blessed by God, I promise to protect it from immorality, misuse, and excesses.

(signature) _____

(date) _____

COOKING TOGETHER

Cooking together can be lots of fun and teaches cooperation.

A "create-your-own-pizza" party allows each student to decide what a pizza should have on it. It encourages creativity as students make their personal pizzas any shape. It demands cooperation as they share equipment and exercise restraint in the number of toppings they use. You may prefer to have them work in teams, creating the ultimate pizza for their team.

Your group might enjoy making pretzels for a fund-raising project or just for the fun of making and eating them together. The pretzel was originally created by fifth century German bakers. At that time, people did not eat meat or dairy products during Lent; they ate bread instead. The bakers decided to make a bread that was good to eat and had religious significance. The crossed arms of the pretzel were intended to represent a Christian at prayer with his palms on his shoulders in a crisscross. You might wish to print this information on slips of paper to add to bagged pretzels that you sell.

A cookie bake can be a Christmas project, but needn't be limited to the holidays. How about a May Day cookie bake or an All Saints' Day cookie bake? Take cookies to a nursing home, shut-in members of your church family, to a children's home, or to an institution for the mentally disabled. It's usually a good idea to arrange for the visits ahead of time, but the cheer of home-baked cookies is almost always welcomed. If you're visiting individuals, consider their health problems and provide special treats for those who cannot eat sugar.

 SS3831

"CREATE-YOUR-OWN PIZZA" PARTY

The following dough recipe is very forgiving if overworked and allows creativity as junior highers create shapes for their pizzas, such as their initials, crosses, or wheels. If time is short, you might prefer to use sliced French bread or prepared pizza breads.

The pizza party isn't just for fun, but that's the main emphasis. Encourage cooperation by asking students to make pizzas by teams. They can be creative, but be prepared for the kid that eats only cheese or vegetables. Make certain they understand that they are to eat what they make, so the food is not wasted. You will need to know how many will be at the "create-your-own-pizza" party so you will have enough of each ingredient.

You may wish to make the dough before the students arrive, or you may have them make it. It isn't necessary to let the dough rise twice. One recipe will make one large pizza (to feed three moderate eaters or two big eaters) or three individual pizzas. The dough may be used for thin or thick crust pizzas.

Toppings you should have on hand:

Pizza sauce (or spaghetti sauce)	Canned mushrooms
Lots of grated mozzarella cheese	Garlic salt
Cooked hamburger	Oregano
Pepperoni	Crushed pineapple
Sliced ham	Sauerkraut
Cooked sausage	Sliced onions
Sliced green peppers	Olives
Canadian bacon	Variety of other cheeses

PIZZA DOUGH

Mix together and let stand for five minutes:
    1 cup lukewarm water
    1 pkg. yeast
    (Or use quick-rising yeast and forget the wait.)
Add:
    1 tsp. sugar
    1 tsp. salt
    1 tbsp. shortening
Mix well. Add a cup at a time until it forms a stiff dough:
    3 cups flour
Pat or roll out into a thin or thick crust. Add toppings. Bake approximately 25 minutes at 425 degrees. Baking time varies greatly due to thinness of crust and thickness of toppings added.

SOFT PRETZELS

This recipe makes 25 to 30 pretzels.
   2 pkgs. quick-rise yeast
   $\frac{1}{2}$ cup sugar
   2 tsp. salt
   7 cups flour
   2 cups warm water
   1 egg (at room temperature)
   $\frac{1}{4}$ cup soft margarine
   1 egg yolk
   2 tbsp. water
   Coarse salt

Dough can be prepared ahead of time by teacher or parents.

Mix yeast, sugar, and salt into 3 cups of flour. Add beaten egg to warm water. Add egg, water, and $\frac{1}{4}$ cup soft margarine to flour mixture. Beat until well blended. Gradually add the remaining flour to form stiff dough. Knead dough on floured board for 8-10 minutes. Place in a greased bowl and turn to grease top. Cover tightly and refrigerate 2-24 hours.

Place dough on floured board and divide into 25-30 equal parts. Roll each piece of dough into a 20" rope. Shape each rope into a pretzel shape. Place on greased baking sheet. Combine egg yolk and 2 tbsp. water. Brush pretzels with water/yolk mixture. Sprinkle with coarse salt. Allow to rise in warm place until doubled in size (about 30 minutes). Bake 15 minutes at 400 degrees or until golden brown. Remove from baking sheets and cool on wire racks.

SS3831

MOLDED COOKIE DOUGH

Combine the following ingredients in a large bowl and mix thoroughly by hand or with an electric mixer that has a dough hook.

    8-oz. package of completely softened cream cheese
    $1\frac{1}{2}$ cups butter or margarine completely softened
    $1\frac{1}{2}$ cups brown sugar
    1 tsp. salt
    3 tsp. vanilla, almond, rum, lemon, or peppermint flavoring

Or divide the above mixture into three parts, adding 1 tsp. of flavoring, and food coloring if desired, to each.

Add flour gradually, mixing by hand, until mixture forms a ball. $1\frac{2}{3}$ cups flour to each of three parts or 5 cups total.

Knead dough on floured surface, adding a little more flour until dough is smooth, pliable, and not sticky. This dough actually becomes easier to shape the more it is handled. There is no change necessary for high altitude cooking. Makes lots.

Shape it. It may be rolled $\frac{1}{4}$" thick and cut with cookie cutters. You may cut it into almost any shape with a knife, attaching pieces together by moistening dough with a little water. Dough may be made to look like hair by pressing some through a clean garlic press. Add texture or initials, using a toothpick or the end of a straw. It can be rolled into $\frac{1}{2}$" thick ropes and shaped into initials, bells, hearts, etc. Make the dough into tiny pies by cutting it into circles, placing 1 tbsp. of prepared pie filling in the center of one circle and covering it with a second circle, sealing the edges.

Decorate it. You may wish to firmly press nuts, raisins, chocolate sprinkles, cinnamon candies, candied fruit, or colored sugars into cookies before baking. Cookies may be painted by mixing a few drops of food coloring in a tablespoon of evaporated milk and painting it on with a clean, unused watercolor brush. Frosting may be added after the cookies cool.

Bake the cookies at 350 degrees until the edges are light brown (10-15 minutes for thin cookies and 15-20 minutes for thicker cookies). Cool five minutes before removing the cookies from the baking sheets. The dough may be kept in the refrigerator for up to two weeks. Allow it to return to room temperature before attempting to shape it.

SS3831

COOKIE BAKE

You may wish to use your own favorite recipes, but the following have been chosen for their uniqueness.

DIABETIC APPLESAUCE COOKIES

1³/₄ cups flour
1/₂ cup margarine
1 tsp. baking soda
1 tsp. cinnamon
1/₂ tsp. nutmeg
1/₄ tsp. cloves

1 tbsp. liquid sweetener
1 egg (beaten)
1 cup applesauce
1 cup oatmeal
1/₃ cup raisins (optional)

Combine dry ingredients in first column. Combine sweetener, beaten egg, and applesauce, and mix thoroughly into dry ingredients. Mix in oatmeal and raisins. Drop by teaspoonfuls onto a greased cookie sheet. Bake at 375 degrees for 15 minutes or until golden brown. Cooled cookies must be stored in refrigerator.

NO-FAIL FUDGE

1/₂ lb. American cheese spread (Velveeta™)
1/₂ lb. margarine
1 tsp. vanilla

2 lbs. powdered sugar
1/₂ cup cocoa
Nuts

Lightly grease a 9" x 13" pan. Melt margarine and cheese together. Add vanilla. Mix cocoa and powdered sugar and stir into melted mixture. Beat well. Add nuts. Spread in pan and chill before cutting.

GINGERBREAD MEN

Combine 1 cup each of sugar, oil, molasses, and hot water. Add 2 eggs. Mix well and add 1 tsp. baking soda, 1/₂ tsp. salt, 1 heaping tsp. ginger, and 1 tsp. cinnamon. Mix all ingredients well and add 6 to 7 cups of flour (1/₃ of flour may be whole wheat). When dough is smooth and pliable, roll it on a floured board and cut with cookie cutters. (Or form the body and head from two balls of dough, attach arms and legs of dough rolled into ropes, flatten whole figure, and draw features with a nutpick.) Bake at 350 degrees for 10-15 minutes or until golden brown.

LEMON SUGAR SNAPS

1/₂ cup margarine
1 cup sugar
1 egg
2 tsp. grated lemon peel or 1 tsp. lemon extract

2 cups flour
1¹/₂ tsp. baking powder
1/₄ tsp. salt

Cream margarine and sugar. Add egg and lemon peel or extract. Mix together flour, baking powder, and salt. Blend slowly into creamed mixture. Roll 1/₄" thick on well-floured surface and cut into shapes. Place on cookie sheets, sprinkle with sugar, and bake at 375 degrees for 8 minutes or until just starting to brown. Cool on wire racks. Yields about four dozen cookies.

SS3831

DRAMAS

The dramas in this section are based on the two great commandments. "Jesus replied: 'Love the Lord your God with all your heart and with all your soul and with all your mind.' And the second is like it: 'Love your neighbor as yourself.'" (Matthew 22:37, 39) Each theme is portrayed with a short biblical drama and a modern drama. The dramas conclude with thought-provoking questions.

The purpose of drama is to help junior highers see life from the perspective of others by reading their words (or memorizing them) and taking on the persona of different characters to share events in their lives. Dramas need not be acted out; however, to be useful as teaching tools, they may simply be read in parts. The questions following each drama may be used to provoke discussion. The biblical version may be used with the modern version for comparison and to make the biblical version more understandable.

These dramas may be successfully performed before a small group or an entire congregation with just a few props. Or they may be acted out with full costume and props, many of which the students may wish to make themselves. If the dramas are acted out before a large group, students may also wish to challenge the thoughts of the audience by asking them some of the questions.

LOVE THE LORD
Daniel 3

Cast

Shadrach   Abednego   Herald
Meshach   Nebuchadnezzar   Troublemaker
Three guards

Scene

A throne (stage right) faces the furnace entrance across several feet of space. Leave space behind the throne for actors to pass behind it as they leave and enter the scene.

Props

The throne may be an elaborate chair or a plain, high-backed chair covered with a shiny or purple cloth. A furnace may be created by a door opening onto a scene containing a painted image of an idol. The furnace could be two chairbacks with a space between them, or two six-foot stepladders with the space between them bridged by a board. By covering ladders with crepe paper or old blankets, they can be made to represent the legs of a huge idol. You will also need three lengths of rope to wrap around Shadrach, Meshach, and Abednego. Period costumes may be solid-colored bathrobes with sashes. You may wish to design more elaborate costumes as illustrated.

Herald may have a rolled scroll from which he reads his announcement.

Music to summon worshipers may be on a cassette tape.

The guards may carry spears made of broom handles with cardboard spear points.

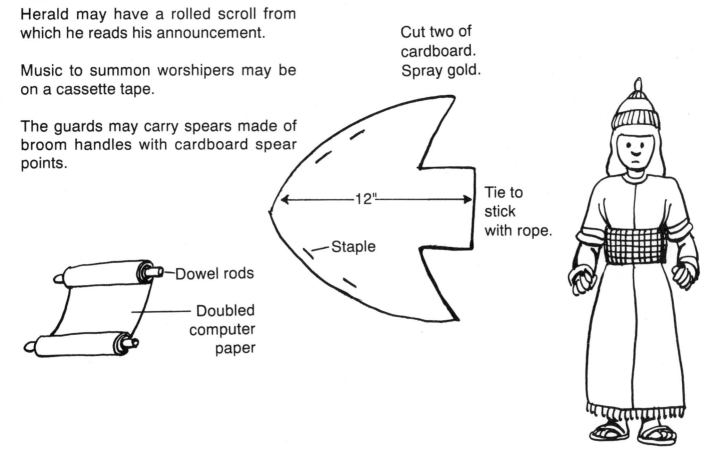

Cut two of cardboard. Spray gold.

12"

Staple

Tie to stick with rope.

Dowel rods

Doubled computer paper

SS3831

NEBUCHADNEZZAR enters from stage right, sits on throne, and admires his newly completed idol.

TROUBLEMAKER enters, standing to right and a little in front of Nebuchadnezzar.

SHADRACH, MESHACH, and ABEDNEGO enter, stopping at stage rear about halfway between idol and Nebuchadnezzar, looking at idol as if not certain what to think.

GUARDS enter and halt to gaze at idol.

HERALD enters, standing upstage at attention just behind Nebuchadnezzar's throne.

NEBUCHADNEZZAR (*To himself*): Well done, well done. They've followed my design beautifully. Our new god has my dignity, my strength of jawline and body. My subjects will not forget whom they worship and who rules them. (*Snaps fingers at Herald, who stiffens to attention*) You know my orders. Announce them.
HERALD: Hear ye! Hear ye! This is what you are commanded to do, O peoples, nations, and men of every language: As soon as you hear the sound of the horn, flute, zither, lyre, harp, pipes, and all kinds of music, you must fall down and worship the image of gold that King Nebuchadnezzar has set up. Whoever does not fall down and worship will immediately be thrown into a blazing furnace.

(Music sounds)

GUARDS, HERALD, and TROUBLEMAKER sink to their knees and bow their heads. (*Be certain Troublemaker can be seen clearly by audience.*) SHADRACH, MESHACH, ABEDNEGO stand together looking from Nebuchadnezzar to the idol.

SHADRACH: There's the music. I feel like I should bow down. Although our people were brought into this land in bondage, the king has treated us well. I am one of his trusted officials. Perhaps I owe it to him to bow to this foolish golden idol.

MESHACH: You can't mean that, Shadrach. Our God has commanded us to worship no other god. These people think of this thing as a god.

ABEDNEGO: I remember the commandment, Meshach, but I don't want to die either.

MESHACH: You can't mean to bow to an idol, Abednego. You would seem to be worshiping it.

ABEDNEGO (*Takes deep breath and looks fearfully at Nebuchadnezzar*): No, I won't bow to it, but I sure wish our God wasn't testing my faith like this. We've been in this land so long, I hardly remember the stories my grandfather told me of our God, but I haven't forgotten the commandments.

SHADRACH: Maybe no one will notice we aren't bowing down. There are thousands of people out here on the plain of Dura.

TROUBLEMAKER (*Lifts head to look at Shadrach, Meshach, Abednego, then speaks to audience*): Here's my chance to show up those Jews who think they are so smart. They came here as captives and now they are trying to take over everything. They are stealing important official positions from my own people and those who deserve them more. We don't want their kind here. (*Music sounds and he stands up with Herald and Guards, then bows before king.*)

Your Majesty, I beg leave to tell you that the idol you have created is magnificent. All your subjects gladly bow to the image, which has a hint of your majestic face and form. Everyone bowed down to it, that is except . . . uh . . . except . . . .

NEBUCHADNEZZAR (*Leans forward and demands angrily*): Who dares defy my command? Speak up, man.

TROUBLEMAKER: Well, your Majesty, those three Jews over there didn't even nod their heads, much less fall to their knees. They have important positions in your government, your Majesty. By not bowing down they are setting a bad example for your other subjects.

NEBUCHADNEZZAR: How dare they defy my commands! Guards, bring those three men to me immediately. (*Guards bring Shadrach, Meshach, and Abednego to king, who looks them over and seems surprised.*) I know you three men. I appointed you as provincial leaders. You have served me well in the past. Is it true that you now refuse to serve my gods or worship this wonderful image of gold I have set up?

SHADRACH (*Looks hopefully at Meshach and Abednego, and answers when they don't*): Yes, it is true, your Majesty. We do not bow down to idols or serve your gods.

MESHACH: We are worshippers of the one true God, your Majesty. Our God commands us to serve no other god.

ABEDNEGO (*Clenches shaking hands in front of him*): May I remind you that you have not refused us the right to worship as we wish in the past, your Majesty?

SS3831

NEBUCHADNEZZAR: You three are being foolish. You are my subjects now. You will do as I command. I'll give you another chance and have the music sounded again. If you fall down and worship the image I made, we'll forget about this. But if you do not worship it, you will be thrown immediately into a blazing furnace. I doubt that your god will be able to rescue you from my power then.

MESHACH: Your Majesty, we don't need to defend ourselves before you. If we are thrown into the blazing furnace, the God we serve will rescue us from your hand, O king.

ABEDNEGO: And even if our God doesn't save us, we want you to know, your Majesty, that we will not serve your gods or worship the image of gold you have set up.

NEBUCHADNEZZAR (*So furious he stands up*): No one defies me! Make the furnace seven times hotter than usual, tie up these men, and throw them into the flames.

(*The king sits down as Guards wrap ropes around Shadrach, Meshach, and Abednego [Allow the three captives to hold ends of ropes as if they are tied] and shoves them toward furnace entrance. Guards prod them through furnace opening with spears and collapse as if killed by heat. Shadrach, Meshach, and Abednego allow ropes they were holding around themselves to fall to floor as they wander around, looking as if interested in inside of furnace.*)

FURNACE

NEBUCHADNEZZAR (*Holds hand over eyes as if peering into bright flames*): Weren't there only three men that we tied up and threw into the fire?

TROUBLEMAKER (*Looks into furnace and steps back in surprise*): Yes, there were only three, oh king.

NEBUCHADNEZZAR: Then why do I see four men walking around in the fire now? They have no bonds on them and they seem unharmed. Look at that fourth man. He looks like a son of the gods. (*Snaps fingers at Herald*) Go get them all and bring them to me.

HERALD (*Stops well away from furnace opening and shouts*): Shadrach, Meshach, and Abednego, servants of the Most High God, come out of there! Come here to me and bring your friend! (*As Shadrach, Meshach, and Abednego leave furnace, Herald looks inside for fourth man, then sniffs at their clothing as he leads them to the king.*) How odd. They don't even smell of smoke.

TROUBLEMAKER (*Walks around Shadrach, Meshach, and Abednego*): I can't understand this. Their clothes aren't scorched. The hair on their heads isn't even singed. And who was that fourth man?

NEBUCHADNEZZAR (*Sits stiffly on his throne as he proclaims*): Praise be to the God of Shadrach, Meshach, and Abednego, who has sent His angel to rescue His servants! You trusted in Him and defied my command. You were willing to give up your lives rather than serve or worship any god except your own God. I decree that from this time forward any people of any nation who dare say anything against the God of Shadrach, Meshach, and Abednego will be cut into pieces and their houses will be turned into piles of rubble, for no other god can save his servants as your God has saved you.

TROUBLEMAKER (*Moving off stage*): I think I'd better disappear for awhile. This didn't work out at all as I'd hoped. Why didn't they burn up? Whoever heard of a God that could save His people like that? I'd better be more careful in the future when I try to get rid of these Jews with their powerful God.

NEBUCHADNEZZAR: You three have served your God well. I expect you to serve me with as much courage as you serve your God. I am giving you promotions. You may go.

Exit everyone except NEBUCHADNEZZAR and HERALD, who stands just behind his chair. The king thoughtfully admires his idol for several seconds.

HERALD (*To audience*): The God of these three must be the one true God. How can I worship this golden image if the true God says people must worship only Him? (*Wags head uncertainly as Nebuchadnezzar stands up.*)

NEBUCHADNEZZAR and HERALD exit.

SS3831

THOUGHTS TO CONSIDER

1. If you had been Shadrach, Meshach, or Abednego, would you have had enough faith in God to risk your life and defy the king?

2. Do you believe it is possible for God to save people from certain death, such as in a furnace?

3. Why do you think Nebuchadnezzar thought the fourth man in the fire looked like a son of the gods?

4. Do you know people like the Troublemaker, who hate people because they are of another religion and race?

5. Did Shadrach, Meshach, and Abednego do anything to harm the Troublemaker?

6. The Bible says the love of money is the root of all evil. How do you think money can be an idol that people worship?

7. What other things do people place above God?

8. Why didn't Shadrach, Meshach, and Abednego bow down and pretend to worship the idol even if they really weren't doing it?

9. Would you have considered pretending to worship the idol to save your life?

SS3831

THE "IN" CROWD

Cast

Tracy	Pat	Billy	Mike
Lee	Mel	Andy	Charlie

All parts may be played by boys or girls since these could be nicknames for either sex.

Scene

This is a one-scene skit with some of the action taking place in a clubhouse and some outside the clubhouse.

Props

The characters should wear what they normally wear to school. The clubhouse wall may be anything that lends itself to separating the scene in two, with the clubhouse to the left and the area outside it to the right. In the clubhouse there is a table with an image or statue of some kind on it. Around the image are a new flashlight, a package of pencils, and a few other packaged toys and school supplies. A few chairs are scattered around inside the clubhouse where students with nonspeaking parts and some of the main characters may sit.

MIKE, LEE, MEL, and CHARLIE enter clubhouse from stage left. They sit or stand around, saying nothing. MEL is sitting. TRACY, PAT, and BILLY enter from stage right and stop outside clubhouse.

TRACY (*Excited*): Can you believe it? I've always wanted to be in the Aces. I can't believe they asked all three of us at the same time.

PAT: I don't know, Tracy. We've been friends for a long time. Do we really need to be in a club?

BILLY: Don't be like that, Pat. Of course we want to be Aces. They're the best club in school.

ANDY (*Enters from stage right and joins TRACY, PAT, and BILLY*): I'm glad to see you all came. I wasn't sure you would. I kind of thought Pat would talk you out of it.

PAT: I like having fun as much as the next person.

TRACY: Sure we want to be Aces, Andy. You're the best club at school.

ANDY: Well, come on in the clubhouse and meet everybody.

BILLY (*Pauses to admire building before entering it*): This is a really neat clubhouse.

ANDY: Charlie's parents had it built for him when he was a little kid. They're cool. They think kids need privacy, so they don't bother us. Fact is, I don't even know what they look like. They aren't home a lot.

SS3831

Tracy, Andy, Billy, and Pat enter clubhouse and exchange greetings with others.

PAT (*Looks at figure on table*): What's this thing?

MIKE (*Pats figure on head*): This is our High Ace, what else? Charlie's dad brought it back from somewhere, and we decided to make it our good luck charm. It's cool, isn't it?

BILLY: It looks like some kind of idol or something. What's that stuff around it?

MEL (*Stands and moves to table*): That's the stuff we collect for the good luck charm. I mean, what's an idol without a few sacrifices?

TRACY: Sacrifices? I don't get it.

MEL: It means, if you really want to be an Ace, you gotta go to a store and rip something off. (*Looks at stuff on table and frowns*) And it better be better than this junk too. We haven't kept up our standards lately.

BILLY: You've got to be kidding. You don't expect us to steal something just so we can join your club. My folks would kill me if I got caught shoplifting!

LEE: If you want to be an Ace, you have to steal something. That's the way it is. If you can't do it, you're nobody.

CHARLIE: Hey, guys, it's really neat to be an Ace. You've always got friends you can count on.

MIKE (*Looks from Tracy to Pat to Billy*): That's the way it is. If you want to be an Ace, you've got to rip off something and bring it here for the High Ace.

TRACY: I really do want to be an Ace, Mike, but I don't steal things (*Waves at figure*), not even for some dumb thing like this.

LEE: You guys are chickens. What's the big deal about swiping junk?

PAT: Because it's wrong. Because that isn't what I want from a club. I want friends, not people who can't be trusted.

CHARLIE: Come on, it's no big deal. So we steal some cheap little things from stores. It's not like we can't pay for the things we take. It's the thrill of getting away with it.

BILLY: Do you mean you have to shoplift something more than once? Why?

MIKE: Because we're the best club in school, why do you think? Come on, guys, make up your minds. Either you do what it takes to get initiated, or you can get out of here.

PAT: You know, I go to church.

LEE: Big deal. What's that got to do with anything?

ANDY: I go to church too. My mom or dad drops me off there every Sunday. What's this got to do with church?

PAT: Didn't anyone there ever tell you it's wrong to steal things?

MEL: This is just little stuff. Junk really.

BILLY: Maybe Pat's right. It isn't just that you're stealing things; you're taking them so you can be part of the club. It's like this club is more important than doing the right thing.

LEE: Maybe it is. You guys are real wimps.

TRACY: I thought I really wanted to be an Ace, but Pat's right. It's not worth it. Some things are more important–like being honest.

CHARLIE: But it's really fun being an Ace. All you have to do is rip off something little. You guys are my friends, aren't you? You want to be part of my club, don't you?

ANDY: Yeah, come on, guys. It's no big deal. You're our friends. Don't you want to be part of our club?

PAT: The only way I'd want to be part of your club is if you drop this head Ace stuff and cut out the shoplifting. I like to have fun, not do stupid things.

SS3831

Mike, Lee, Mel, Andy, and Charlie look at one another.

MIKE: If you don't like the way we run our club, then you don't have to join. We like it the way it is.

PAT: Fine with me. No club is as important as you want me to think this one is. (*Walks out of clubhouse followed by Tracy*)

BILLY (*Follows Pat and Tracy after a few seconds*): How'd you ever have the guts to do that, Pat? I'm not sure I could.

PAT(*Stops and turns to Billy*): You just did. You didn't have to follow me. I was speaking only for myself.

TRACY: Well, you're right. I never knew they thought they were so great they could do things like that. (*Sighs*) But now Charlie and Andy will never speak to me again.

BILLY: I hate to think what they're going to tell everyone about us at school.

PAT (*Slowly walks off stage followed by Tracy and Billy*): Does it really matter what they say about us? We did what we knew was right. I'm not going to beg them to take me back. It may not be cool to talk about God, but I'll take Him any day over the Aces.

SS3831

THOUGHTS TO CONSIDER

1. Do you think you could tell the members of a club you really wanted to join that they were wrong?

2. Do you think that in a way the Aces are worshiping the High Ace?

3. Do you think that in a way they were worshiping the club?

4. How is the High Ace like Nebuchadnezzar's idol?

5. Are there other things a person can want so badly that they seem almost like idols? Name brand clothes? Video games?

6. Do you think Charlie and Andy want to be Aces, or are they members just to have friends? Does it make sense to do something against your principles just to belong?

7. Why didn't Tracy, Pat, and Billy just buy something and pretend to have stolen it so they could be Aces?

SS3831

THE GOOD SAMARITAN
Based on Luke 10:30-35

Cast

Two Bandits	Traveler	Levite
Priest	Samaritan	Innkeeper

Scene

A large open area to stage right represents the road to Jericho. To stage left is a wall (edge toward audience) meant to represent the inn. Two cots with feet toward audience are inside inn.

Props

The inn wall may be a bulletin board on coasters or any other object that will represent a wall. The two cots may be pallets of blankets. The cast may wear robes or their everyday clothes with long pieces of cloth thrown over their shoulders and around their waists. The Samaritan should have some kind of cloak and a bag to hold clothing and medical supplies. In his bag, the Samaritan should have two small bottles to represent the wine and oil with which he washes the Traveler's wounds and some lengths of white cloth to use as bandages. The Samaritan also needs several coins (quarters, half dollars, or metal slugs) to pay the Innkeeper. The Traveler should have on a fancy cloak and be carrying a bag. The Innkeeper needs a bowl and cup on a tray.

TRAVELER enters stage right.

TWO BANDITS enter stage left from behind inn, attack Traveler, and run off with his cloak and bag. Traveler is left lying at center right stage.

The PRIEST enters and pauses in surprise to look down at Traveler.

PRIEST (*Aloud to himself*): Why, there's a man on the ground. What's he doing there? His face looks as if he's been beaten, and where is his baggage? Could he have been attacked by bandits? (*Looks around anxiously*) He isn't making any sound, isn't moving. Could he be dead? (*Starts to step nearer, but doesn't*) I should see if I can help him, but (*Again looks anxiously around him*) what if the men who attacked him are still in the area. I have a ceremony to perform. People are expecting me. I don't dare be delayed (*Takes a step away*). Surely someone else will come along soon to see if he can be helped. (*Begins walking away*) Maybe he's dead.

PRIEST exits.

TRAVELER moans loudly and moves around a little but can't seem to get up. Lies still again.

LEVITE enters and pauses in shock to look down at Traveler.

Shining Star Publications, Copyright © 1994

SS3831

LEVITE (*Aloud to himself*): That poor man. (*Moves a little nearer Traveler*) He looks badly hurt. There's blood everywhere. (*Looks at his own hands*) I should try to help him, but I'll almost certainly get his blood on me. Then I'll have to go through the purification rites, and I don't have time for that. I have things I must do. (*Steps back a little*) Surely someone will come along soon who has more time than I for the cleansing rites necessary if they touch this poor man.

LEVITE exits.

SAMARITAN enters and immediately steps forward and kneels beside Traveler.

SAMARITAN: You poor man, you're badly hurt. (*Talks soothingly as he takes bottles and bandages from bag, cleans Traveler's wounds, and bandages his arm and head*) I see you are a Jew. I really hope you don't wake up while I tend your wounds. I'm not certain what you'll do when you discover that I'm a Samaritan. I suspect your people hate mine even more than mine hate yours. It's all so foolish, really. We both worship the same God.

TRAVELER moves a little, groans, and mutters something.

SAMARITAN: You seem to have been attacked by bandits. I'll take you to an inn and stay with you for the night until you're feeling better. Do you think you can stand?

SAMARITAN helps Traveler to his feet, wraps his robe around the wounded man, drapes Traveler's uninjured arm around his neck, and helps the injured man hobble across the stage to lie down on cot inside inn. Samaritan lies down on second cot. Both appear to sleep. Samaritan gets up at sound of a knock on door.

INNKEEPER (*Enters carrying tray with bowls and cups*): This is the meal you ordered last night, Samaritan. Are you going to be staying here much longer?

SAMARITAN: Actually I need to leave immediately. I was expected in Jericho last night.

INNKEEPER: What about your friend on the bed there? He looks injured.

SAMARITAN (*Picks up bag and smiles at Traveler before saying to Innkeeper*): He seems to be feeling better now, but I don't really know him. He was attacked by bandits yesterday. (*Takes coins from pocket or bag and hands them to Innkeeper*) This should be enough to pay for his food and lodging until he is well enough to travel. If it isn't, I'll be back in a few days and pay you what else he owes.

SAMARITAN exits carrying bag.

INNKEEPER (*Helps Traveler sit up and places tray on his lap*): You're a Jew, aren't you?

TRAVELER: Yes, I'm a Jew.

INNKEEPER: What are you doing with that Samaritan? Don't you know just touching him makes you unclean?

TRAVELER: If he hadn't been willing to touch me, I'd be dead. That man has more goodness in him than the Priest and Levite who left me for dead. The Priest was afraid of the Bandits and didn't want to be delayed, and the Levite didn't have time for purification rites.

INNKEEPER (*Gazes in direction Samaritan exited*): Why do you think he did it, took care of you I mean?

TRAVELER: I'm not really sure, but I know he has a more loving heart than anyone else I met on the road to Jericho or anywhere else, for that matter.

INNKEEPER: Perhaps you'd feel better if you sat in the sun in the courtyard.

INNKEEPER helps TRAVELER to feet and they exit.

SS3831

THOUGHTS TO CONSIDER

1. Could the Priest have been considered irresponsible by the people who were waiting for him if he had stopped to help and had also been attacked by the Bandits?

2. Jews were considered ritually unclean if they got the blood of another person on them. A rather complicated purification ceremony was necessary before they were once again able to return to their normal lives. If the Traveler had died while the Levite was tending his wounds, the purification ceremony would have been even more complicated. Even if the Levite did have important things to do, did that justify him ignoring someone who needed his help?

3. Why do you think the Samaritan helped the Traveler even when people of his own kind ignored his need?

4. Do you think helping the Traveler was more difficult for the Samaritan when he knew the man would despise him if he were conscious?

5. Jesus doesn't say anything about how the Traveler felt about all this. Could he have been angry at the Samaritan for making him ritually unclean by helping him?

6. Do you think it's possible for people to be so wrapped up in their prejudices that they resent people who try to help them?

7. Have you ever tried to do something nice for someone and been misunderstood?

 SS3831

IS THAT MY NEIGHBOR?

Cast

Mugger 1	Victim	Business Executive
Mugger 2	Police Officer	Hospital Clerk
Student		

Scene

To stage left is an area separated from the rest of the scene by something suggesting a wall with an entrance sign that reads "Emergency Clinic." Center stage right is something representing a doorway with a sign over it that suggests it is a well-to-do business, such as Fine Jewelry, Stockbrokers, or Boutique.

Props

The clinic should have a wheelchair (or cot) and a desk. The Hospital Clerk needs a clipboard with some papers, a pen, and a wastebasket. The Police Officer needs something about his costume to suggest he is an officer (perhaps a badge). The Business Executive should have a briefcase and a watch. The Victim should wear a nice coat and some jewelry, and carry a shopping bag. The Student should have a backpack with some books in it and a billfold with something that looks like money in it. You also need a symbol of hatred, such as a KKK hood, a swastika pendant, a tattoo drawn in marker, or whatever object will suggest hatred for the racial or ethnic group to which the Student belongs.

VICTIM enters from stage right, walking quickly with head down and clutching shopping bag.

MUGGERS enter from stage left, attack Victim, steal coat, jewelry, and shopping bag, and run away stage right.

VICTIM lies as if dead, stage front right.

BUSINESS EXECUTIVE comes out of door marked with name of business, locks door, then notices Victim on sidewalk. Cautiously moves a little nearer Victim.

SS3831

BUSINESS EXECUTIVE (*Aloud to himself*): What's he doing here? I haven't seen a homeless person out here before. (*Looks Victim over more carefully without touching him*) He dresses pretty well for a derelict. I wonder if someone hit him or if he fell down. Maybe he's just drunk, but what if he's really hurt? I suppose I ought to call 911, but I promised Bill I'd meet him at six. (*Looks at watch*) If I call for an ambulance I'd have to explain who this guy is and how he got here, and I don't know. I didn't see or hear a thing, so how do I explain that? The clinic is just down the street. Maybe he'll come to and walk down there on his own, if he's really hurt. (*Takes a step away from Victim*) What if I hurt him more by trying to move him? He could sue me. (*Takes another step away*) Actually, he looks dead. I'd never be able to explain that. (*Hurries away*)

BUSINESS EXECUTIVE exits stage right. VICTIM moans loudly, moves about as if trying to sit up, and falls back to lie still.

POLICE OFFICER (*Enters and stops, looks down at Victim, shakes head, and sighs*): Not another one. It seems like all I ever see anymore is derelicts. (*Looks a little more closely*) This one looks kind of beat up. His clothes look pretty good though. (*Shakes head again*) What can we do with so many people who have no place to go, no work, no reason to live, or so it seems? (*Touches Victim with toe*) Come on, fellow. Let's get up and get a move on. I don't want to have to haul you in for . . . for . . . whatever. I don't want to even think about the paperwork if I have to do something with you. Come on. You'll freeze out here if you don't get up. Don't be dead, buddy. That's even more paperwork. (*Looks offstage to right*) What's that?

POLICE OFFICER exits running, stage right.

STUDENT (*Enters and goes immediately to kneel beside Victim*): Boy, you have really been kicked around. There's an emergency clinic just down the street if we can get you there. Do you think you could stay on your feet if I help you up? (*Victim moves a little and mumbles something*) I'll try not to hurt you. (*Student removes his backpack and coat*) You're so cold. (*Helps Victim sit up and wraps coat around him*) Maybe that will help. (*Helps victim to feet*) Hey, what's this? It must have fallen out of your pocket. (*Holds up symbol of hatred so audience can see it*) Well, I guess if you were feeling OK, you wouldn't want anything to do with me! (*Student helps Victim hobble to emergency clinic and sits him in wheelchair, or helps him lie on cot*) They'll take better care of you here than I can.

HOSPITAL CLERK (*Enters and looks down at Victim while confronting Student*): Did you bring this man in here?

                                     SS3831

STUDENT: Yes, I did.

HOSPITAL CLERK: Do you want to tell me his name and what happened to him?

STUDENT (*Looks at Victim, sighs, and pulls billfold from pocket*): I've only got about $150. I was saving it to buy a bicycle so I could get to class on time but, (*Offers clerk money*) why don't you use it for him? He can't go back out in the cold tonight, and his injuries need to be treated. I'll come back to see how he is tomorrow. If you need more money, I will try to figure out a way to get it if he isn't ready to be out on his own.

HOSPITAL CLERK (*Looks at money and then at Student*): Is this some kind of joke? You're giving me money to take care of a stranger? People just don't do that, not in this day and age.

STUDENT: He needs it more than I do. I hope he gets better soon, but I need to get out of here before he's completely conscious. I don't think he'd like me much.

HOSPITAL CLERK: You're not making any sense.

STUDENT: This is his. (*Hands symbol of hatred to Clerk*) Give it to him when he's conscious. I've got to be going. I'm late for class.

STUDENT exits hurriedly.

VICTIM (*Sighs loudly and perks up*): Where am I? What happened?

HOSPITAL CLERK: You're at an emergency clinic. The person who brought you in said this is yours. (*Hands him the symbol of hatred*) Did you get a good look at your Good Samaritan?

VICTIM (*Sighs heavily again*): Yes. (*Looks at symbol, shakes head, and tosses symbol into wastebasket*) I don't get it. Why did he do that for me? He saw that. He knows how I feel. Other people saw me lying there in the gutter and didn't do a thing to help me. I could hear them, but I was too stunned to move. I was too out of it to tell them that somebody mugged me and I needed help. So why was he nice to me? What's in it for him?

HOSPITAL CLERK (*Shows money to Victim*): There's nothing in it for him. It cost him $150 to be certain we kept you here overnight.

VICTIM: He didn't need to do that. I've got money. I hate owing someone, especially someone like that.

HOSPITAL CLERK: You should be glad someone like "that" came along or you'd still be out there freezing to death in the street. I'd better get you into one of the examination rooms.

CLERK exits, pushing Victim or helping him walk.

SS3831

THOUGHTS TO CONSIDER

1. What would you do if you found someone in the gutter and didn't know how he had gotten there? Would you react instantly, or would you consider the consequences and dangers first? Why might it be wiser to use a few seconds to consider these things before you do anything?

2. Did the Business Executive have a reason to fear helping the Victim? Could you be sued for trying to help someone? (Note: Some states have Good Samaritan Laws especially for this purpose, but not all do.)

3. What do you think motivated the Student to come to the Victim's aid?

4. Why do you think the Student continued to aid the Victim even when he realized he was someone the Victim would despise?

5. Why do people hate other people?

6. How can you overcome your own prejudices and help others to overcome theirs?

7. Could you give up money you'd saved for something for yourself because you thought someone else had a greater need of it?

8. Do you think there really are people like the Student around?

9. Why did the Victim resent the goodness of the Student?

10. Do you think people today are more prejudiced or less prejudiced than they were in Jesus' time? In the time of Jesus, Samaritans and Jews hated each other so much that a Jew would walk dozens of miles out of his way to avoid setting foot in Samaria. Samaritans disliked Jews just as much.

11. Is it easier or harder to help someone today than it was in the time of Jesus?

"WHAT IS LOVE?" DIALOGUE

The purpose of this dialogue is to direct junior highers in their understanding of the many aspects of love. At their ages they think often of romance and sex and may think that this is what love is all about. "What Is Love?" will help them understand that there are many forms of love and all of them are acceptable to God when properly applied. It also helps them see the evidence of love through actions.

"What Is Love?" may be used as a lesson which students read in parts and discuss. Some thoughts and questions to encourage discussion follow the script. The Leader's part should be read by an adult since it is an adult point of view. Be prepared for difficult questions, possibly some embarrassing ones. You don't need to answer personal questions, and your students should not be prodded or teased into revealing personal details they do not wish to divulge. Work to maintain an open attitude, one in which profitable discussion can take place.

"What Is Love?" may also be used as part of a youth service in your church. It makes an excellent sermonette for Valentine's Day, but may be used effectively at any time of year. Before "What Is Love?" is performed, students should read through it as a group and discuss it so they understand what they are saying.

The only props necessary are valentines or greeting cards. A Bible may be used by Speaker A. "What Is Love?" has been written for twelve students and one adult, but some parts may be read by the same person. To cut the number of participants down to six students and one adult: A may also read G. B can read K. C can read I. D can read L. E can read H. F can read J. Junior highers should be encouraged to memorize their parts so they can speak as if they are having a conversation. Some students may need notes to prompt them in their parts. If you have more than twelve in your group, extras may join the scene to nod or agree aloud or disagree as needed. They can laugh too. A dipstick for love is a funny idea and E and H are trying for comedy.

                                                                      SS3831

SPEAKER A (*As if reading from a Bible*): "If I speak in the tongues of man and of angels, but have not love, I am only a resounding gong or a clanging cymbal. If I have the gift of prophecy and can fathom all mysteries and all knowledge, and if I have a faith that can move mountains, but have not love, I am nothing. If I give all I possess to the poor and surrender my body to the flames, but have not love, I gain nothing. Love is patient, love is kind. It does not envy, it does not boast, it is not proud. It is not rude, it is not self-seeking, it is not easily angered, it keeps no record of wrongs. Love does not delight in evil but rejoices with the truth. It always protects, always trusts, always hopes, always perseveres. Love never fails." (1 Corinthians 13:1-8a)

SPEAKER B: Those are beautiful words, but I'm not sure I understand them.

LEADER: In his first letter to the Christians at Corinth, Paul was concerned with relationships, especially those within this church in a pretty wild city. He wanted those Christians to understand that the spiritual gifts they received from God were useless if love didn't motivate their use of them. From his definition of love, it is clear that Paul believed love in its many aspects can be a very positive force in the life of every person.

SPEAKER C: My sister's boyfriend is very jealous. He gets mad if he sees her talking to another guy. They really love each other. They're planning to get married. So, why is he so jealous?

SPEAKER D: Maybe because he doesn't love her enough to trust her. I think, if you love someone, you will trust that person completely, but that doesn't have anything to do with what we're talking about. The Bible doesn't talk about romantic love. It only talks about loving God and our neighbors. Right?

SS3831

LEADER: Sorry, but I can't agree with that. The Tree of Knowledge in the Garden of Eden wasn't just a symbol of man's relationship with God, but also the relationship between man and woman. Remember, Adam and Eve were told by God to be fruitful and multiply. God blessed their sexuality. The Song of Songs, written by King Solomon, seems to be a collection of marriage poems. It praises the wonders of sexual love, but with an emphasis on the understanding and devotion on which that love is based. The New Testament concentrates mainly on God's love for the people He created, their love for Him, and of the New Testament that brought marriage into the early Christian church as a relationship sanctified by God.

SPEAKER E: How do we know if we are loved, or if we love someone else? It would be a lot easier if we had a dipstick for love. Then we'd know if we were low, half empty, or filled up all the way.

SPEAKER F (*Holds up a fan of valentines or greeting cards*): This is how I know how much I'm loved. All my friends and family know that I expect valentines to prove they love me.

SPEAKER G: You mean, if they don't send you valentines, you don't think they love you?

SPEAKER F: Well, they don't love me as much as they should. When you love someone, you prove it by the things you do for that person.

SPEAKER G: Something's wrong with that reasoning, but I'm not sure what. Do we have to give things to someone just to prove our love?

LEADER: Actually that's a tricky question. In the Old Testament we are told that if we love God, we will keep His commandments. That includes not harming our neighbors. The Old Testament doesn't, however, tell us what to do for our neighbors. In the New Testament the emphasis is somewhat changed. We are told that, as Christians, we are known by what we do. Love is genuine goodwill that puts first the needs and interests of the ones we love. That suggests actually doing something about our love.

SPEAKER G: So we *do* need to do things for people and give them things to prove we love them?

SS3831

LEADER: That's not exactly what I'm saying. In the Middle Ages the idea of love producing something was translated to mean that people could earn God's love and a place in heaven by their good works. They got to the point where they were buying something called an "indulgence" which guaranteed that any wrong they might commit was forgiven before they did it. The Reformation changed that, but that doesn't mean doing good for others is bad. There's a fine line between doing something because it comes from the heart and doing it because it is expected as "proof" of our love.

SPEAKER F (*Looks uncertainly at valentines*): These cards are so neat. Do you mean they don't prove anything? How will I know if someone loves me if they don't give me things to prove it?

LEADER: You have to trust in God's love and in the love of people, expecting some kind of physical proof. If someone forgets to give you something or God doesn't answer your prayer, that doesn't mean God or your friend loves you less. Don't confuse love with the things you receive. Love is a lot more than that. A person can have a lot of possessions and not be loved.

SPEAKER H: But I wouldn't say no to a sports car, a condo, or a million dollars.

SPEAKER I: Who would? But I can see how love is more important. Things go away, but real love lasts. Isn't that what the verse says? Love never fails.

SPEAKER J: But love can't be eternal. We all die.

SPEAKER K: Death won't end our love for God because we'll be joining Him in heaven. And our love for our family and friends doesn't have to end when we die either. If you think about it, as long as they live they will remember that we loved them. In that way our love for them will last until they all die too.

SIGH!

SS3831

SPEAKER L: But none of them will live forever. Only God's love is forever. I think those verses in 1 Corinthians are about our love for God. He expects us to use the gifts He gives us for everyone, and we should try harder to like people, even if we can't love some of them. Since God is patient with us, I think we should be patient, even when we don't get what we pray for. It only makes sense we shouldn't act like we think we're better than other people just because we're Christians. I guess we also shouldn't be angry with God when things happen to us that we don't like. But you know, God really expects a lot of us if we love Him.

LEADER: That's true. And we expect a lot of Him, because He loves us. It's the same with our neighbors and those we romantically love as well. Love isn't something that just happens and then sticks to us like glue. It's not like a suit of clothing we can take off and put on when we feel like it. It's something we have to work at, something we live every minute of our lives. Love is a force that both initiates and maintains relationships, not only between people, but also between God and the people He created. Christ taught His disciples, and us, that love created the universe and watches over it; that sacrificial love is expected of those who serve God; that mutual love is the eternal mark of life in God's kingdom.

SS3831

THOUGHTS TO CONSIDER

1. How did God "prove" His love for us?

2. How can we "prove" our love for Him?

3. How can we "prove" our love for families and friends?

4. What is the difference between the love your parents feel for you and the love they feel for each other?

5. Is sex a proof of love?

6. When you truly love someone, do you love him because of something he has done or because of who he is?

7. Can love be earned?

8. Think of some people you love. Why do you love them?

9. Can anger or jealousy make you stop loving someone?

10. If you love someone, you want what is best for that person, not what you think is best for you. How do you think this would affect a boyfriend/girlfriend relationship?